# The City

# Key Concepts series

# The City

Deborah Stevenson

polity

First published in 2013 by Polity Press

Polity Press
65 Bridge Street
Cambridge CB2 1UR, UK

Polity Press
350 Main Street
Malden, MA 02148, USA

ISBN-13: 978-0-7456-4889-7
ISBN-13: 978-0-7456-4890-3(pb)

A catalogue record for this book is available from the British Library.

Typeset in 10.5 on 12 pt Sabon
by Toppan Best-set Premedia Limited
Printed and bound in Great Britain by the MPG Books Group Limited

The publisher has used its best endeavours to ensure that the URLs for external websites referred to in this book are correct and active at the time of going to press. However, the publisher has no responsibility for the websites and can make no guarantee that a site will remain live or that the content is or will remain appropriate.

Every effort has been made to trace all copyright holders, but if any have been inadvertently overlooked the publisher will be pleased to include any necessary credits in any subsequent reprint or edition.

For further information on Polity, visit our website: www.politybooks.com

Dedicated with love to my father Robert
Thomas Smythe (1929–2005)

# Contents

# Plates

All photos are by the author unless otherwise credited.

# Acknowledgements

There are many people who provided friendship and support during the writing of this book. At Polity, Emma Longstaff and Jonathan Skerrett, ably assisted by Lauren Mulholland, were enthusiastic at every stage, first encouraging me to prepare the proposal and then assisting to ensure the timely completion of the manuscript. Production Manager Neil de Cort saw the book through to publication, while copy-editor Justin Dyer worked on the manuscript with considerable care and attention to detail. Thanks are also due to the anonymous reviewers of both the proposal and the manuscript for their probing comments and suggestions.

The book was completed while I was on study leave, and I am very grateful to the University of Western Sydney for giving me this valuable time in which to write. I acknowledge the Australian Research Council for funding two Discovery projects, which informed several chapters of the book: *The City after Dark: The Governance and Lived Experience of Urban Night-Time Culture* (DP0877906, with Stephen Tomsen and David Rowe) and *Places in Transition: A Case Study of Cultural Planning in an Australian City* (LP0454987, with David Rowe and Kevin Markwell).

Sincere thanks go to my colleagues at the Institute for Culture and Society at the University of Western Sydney for providing a welcoming and stimulating work environment, and to Vibha Bhattarai Upadhyay for diligent and engaged research assistance. Melissa Maucort warrants special mention for being a mainstay during my term as Head of the School of Social Sciences. Therese Kenna gave invaluable feedback on an earlier draft of the manuscript and I greatly appreciate her generosity in providing photographs. My thanks also go to: Ien Ang, Lee Artis, Nathaniel Bavinton, Tony Bennett, Lisa Hanlon, Ellen Jordan, Wayne McKenna, Kevin Markwell, Trenton Oldfield and Stephen Tomsen. David Rowe was a constant source of advice and support, as well as a useful photographer and tireless and perceptive co-explorer of the urban. Finally, I thank my family and especially my mother, Nancy, and my sons, Rohan and Cameron, for reality checks and the love that is all too often taken for granted.

*Deborah Stevenson*
*Sydney, 2012*

# Introduction

City life is now the dominant form of existence for most people on the planet, which means that cities are at the centre of the political and economic processes and social relations that shape and define the contemporary world. Cities are sites of anonymity as well as of the most intimate of lived experience – of contradiction and continuity. While for some the world has entered a 'golden age of cities', others argue that the global dominance of the urban is the single biggest threat to social and environmental sustainability at both the micro and the macro levels. In attempting to explain cities, urbanization and urban life, including their rhythms, complexities and consequences, scholars utilize an array of often contradictory theories, concepts and methods. These approaches and frameworks, and the empirical insights they produce, have also variously been used to justify interventions in city building and attempts to manage processes of urban development and shape the lives of urban dwellers. Such interventions, however, and the theories that underpin them, are not value-free. Rather, they are informed, implicitly and explicitly, by particular beliefs about the foundations of knowledge, causality and the nature of the social world. In addition, just as concepts, theories and methods shape academic and professional perspectives on the city, they also influence the character and experience of urbanism.

In order to gain insights into such interrelationships and consequences, and in an effort to appreciate significant urban trends and influences, it is necessary first to probe how the city and urban life have been studied and explained. The starting point for this endeavour is the concept of 'the city' itself and some of the contested and negotiated ways in which it has been understood, used and imagined, including the meanings that are attached to it. It is this challenge that informs the concerns of this book.

Cities and urban culture are of interest to scholars and students across a wide range of social science and humanities disciplines, notably sociology, geography, economics and history. Each field has developed a substantial body of knowledge about aspects of the urban, and scholars ask research questions that are informed by the concerns and orientations of their particular discipline. They bring to their analyses the theories, concepts and methodologies of their subject area, and many debates about the city take place within discipline-specific fora, at particular conferences and in academic journals. As a result, conceptualizations of the city are invariably partial and not uncommonly developed in the absence of a robust engagement with the insights of other disciplines. That said, disciplinary and explanatory silos are also as much reflections and, indeed, outcomes of the vastness and complexity of the urban object as they are indicators of intellectual purity and boundary maintenance.

It was partly in response to what is regarded as the limits of disciplinarity that the field of urban studies emerged to facilitate the multidisciplinary (sometimes interdisciplinary) study and discussion of the city. Significantly, urban studies is not a synthetic field, nor does it necessarily transcend the disciplines; rather, it augments them by providing a space for collaboration and exchange. As Beauregard (2010) notes in his useful survey of urban studies, the 'pull' of the disciplines in the study of the city is strong and many of the most influential contributions to knowledge, and certainly those that are foundational, continue to be grounded in specific subject areas, especially sociology and geography. In addition, and unlike a field such as cultural studies, urban studies is not defined by an identifiable body of theory or set of methodologies. Its purpose, boundaries and object of analysis thus remain 'fuzzy' (Paddison 2001a: x).

Against this backdrop, the current book is sociological in its orientation and aims from this standpoint to address some of the ways in which not only urban sociology but urban studies and the urban disciplines more broadly understand, or contribute to understandings of, the contemporary city. It argues that the most incisive conceptualizations are those that transcend rigid divisions and established dualisms (such as the 'West and the rest', the 'global and the local', the 'rural and the urban') and seek to provide nuanced insights into urban variety and complexity. In commencing this task, the book builds on and engages with significant debates, synthesizes bodies of thought, and draws, when appropriate, on the findings of original research to examine conceptualizations of the city in different national and local contexts as well as different historical and political moments. The book not only reassesses the city and highlights a range of viewpoints, some of which are novel and surprising, but it traces influential concepts and themes in a concise and clearly framed way. It is this combination of synthesis and originality which makes the book suitable for both students and researchers across a range of fields.

The book seeks to draw attention to the significance to cities and urban life of macro processes and systems, including the global movement of ideas, people, goods and practices (and their interconnections), as well as of the personal, the micro and the place-based. The underpinning assumption is that the city is at once conceptual (an idea and the object of theory), material (occupying real space and being formed in response to a range of macro and micro processes) and experienced (lived, sensory and enveloping). Each chapter is self-contained and able to be read in isolation, but important links are made throughout the text between topics and debates, and subtle synthesizing arguments are developed. The book does not present a 'shopping list' of urban theories or a history of urban thought. It is neither exhaustive nor all-encompassing. Rather, it is an engaged work that deals with different 'cuts' into, or ways of approaching, the concept of 'the city'. By taking a thematic approach, it thus introduces readers to a range of significant concerns in the production, reproduction and conceptualization of the city.

The opening chapter identifies some of the most influential foundational frameworks in urban studies, as well as key processes that have either shaped the contemporary metropolis or are salient features of urban life. The importance of theory and method is introduced in the chapter, which recognizes that knowledge about the city is significantly constructed through the methods used to research it. In Chapter 2 the urban consequences of industrialization, 'neoliberalism' and the circulation of capital are considered and several prominent features of contemporary urban landscapes are discussed, including gentrification and the 'new geographies' of wealth and exclusion. Also highlighted are the significant spatial consequences of the current global economic crisis that was triggered by the collapse of the 'subprime' mortgage market in the United States. The most visible urban effects of this crisis include the growing tracts of residential desolation and abandonment.

Chapter 3 examines issues of urban homogeneity, complexity and diversity. In particular, the chapter provides insights into such concerns as suburbanization and the use, and increased privatization of, public space. The chapter suggests that a range of factors, including class, race, gender and age, influence people's presence in public space, and these characteristics are often celebrated as features and evidence of urban diversity and cosmopolitanism; however, they can also be (real and imagined) barriers to public space – both marker and cause of exclusion. The chapter goes on to consider the ways in which creativity, culture and consumption are being mobilized to reshape the metropolis and its uses. The idea of the 'creative city' and the economic and symbolic value being placed on attracting the so-called urban 'creative class' are significant in this context.

It is the intersections of time and space that are central to the concerns of Chapter 4, which looks at the notion of the city at night. The activities that take place in any city after dark play a significant role in shaping the image and liveability of that city and contribute, both positively and negatively, to urban economies. The chapter delves into the main bodies of academic thought that have been influential in explaining and informing both the development and regulation of what has come to be known as the 'night-time economy'. The first of these perspectives emphasizes the goal of stimulating night-time urban space, while the second view is concerned with after-dark criminality and disorderly behaviour and so focuses on processes of regulation, surveillance and policing. The chapter investigates these issues and tensions with reference, in particular, to the United Kingdom and Australia.

Beginning with the proposition that the affective is an important element of contemporary urbanism, Chapter 5 explores what it means to understand the city as the location of the flow and expression of passion and emotion. To this end, the chapter provides a framework for explaining the relationship between emotions and the city, acknowledging that this relationship is multifaceted, socially constructed and located and experienced at the level of the body. Monuments and memorials are significant features of the urban landscape, serving as markers of both power and marginalization as well as being prompts for the expression of collective and private emotion. Cities are also the spaces where religious belief is performed and where the architecture of belief (particularly in the form of places of worship) frequently dominates. The practices associated with religion inform uses of, and movements through, urban space, shaping the rhythms and patterns of travel to and from places of religious significance, including churches, mosques and sites of pilgrimage.

Processes of globalization have transformed cities and their study. Every city is now in some way locked into (or out of) significant global circuits of information, capital, people and ideas. The task of Chapter 6 is to consider some of these circuits and their varying and uneven urban consequences. It is in this context that the complementary ideas of the 'global' and 'world' city gained currency, and the chapter highlights the international flows that have come to define and construct such classifications and associated urban hierarchies. The chapter argues that a significant outcome of globalization and world-global city theses is the 'othering' of those cities that are not part of the primary circuits of economics or influence. These are the 'second cities', the 'small cities' and most cities in the developing world. Indeed, the vast majority of cities are not world or global cities at all. They are, nevertheless, defined in terms of their location *vis-à-vis* the global, and a consequence of the fixation on global networks, hierarchies and processes has been a countervailing interest in these residual or marginalized cities as well as in the 'other' of the global: the local.

Attempts are routinely made to position cities within the various circuits and hierarchies of commerce, tourism and creativity, and often central to these reimaging strategies are major urban development projects focused on former industrial or waterfront sites. Chapter 7 is concerned to probe such urban redevelopment initiatives which operate/come into existence through the circulation of ideas, strategies, people and money. It suggests that city visioning is as much about sameness, universality and predictability as it is about difference and the local. Nevertheless, redevelopment and reimaging projects are located within very specific cities and urban precincts and thus are interpreted and experienced in the context of these spaces. They also function as the zones or territories that connect a city to broader (national, regional, global) financial and other processes and insert it into the itineraries of tourists. Not only are significant global circuits the impetus for building and reshaping urban space, but they are also framing new forms of urban governance, something which many have described in terms of the reassertion of the local. Such processes and initiatives, although global in their scope and influence, have quite varied local consequences that highlight considerable differences among cities. For many cities of the 'third world' or 'global South', for instance, city building is occurring within a 'developmentalist' framework that is being fostered by influential supra-state bodies, such as the World Bank and the agencies of the United Nations.

The concluding chapter brings together the themes and arguments of the book. It closes with a consideration of some emerging challenges in urban studies and urban development, and the continuing utility and sustainability of the concept of the 'city'. In particular, the chapter reiterates the importance of understanding contemporary cities as being formed at the intersection of the real, the imagined and the experienced.

# 1
# Theoretical City

## Concepts and Frameworks

What is the city? How did it come into existence? What processes does it further; what functions does it perform; what purposes does it fulfil? No single definition will apply to all its manifestations and no single description will cover all its transformations, from the embryonic social nucleus to the complex forms of its maturity and the corporeal disintegration of its old age.

Mumford 1989/1961: 3

## Introduction

The question 'what is the city?' is one that has troubled scholars from a range of disciplines from the beginning of the academic study of society. Furthermore, as Mumford suggests in the passage above, it is simply not possible to see or capture the complexity of the city in a single view or to explain it with reference to an all-encompassing theory or set of concepts. In also considering how theories and concepts shape what it is possible to know about cities and urbanism, a recurring theme within urban studies is the continued usefulness of the idea of the city for explaining contemporary urban environments that are sprawling spatial conglomerations cut through with diversity in all its guises and formed through meta structures, processes and trends.

Cities are also comprised of micro sites of formal and informal processes of governance and experience. Some scholars have rejected the idea of the city altogether, arguing that concepts including 'urban', 'postmetropolis', 'multi-centred metropolitan region', 'city-region' and 'megopolis' have more explanatory force and more accurately capture the social and spatial complexity of 'the city'. And yet the idea of 'the city' lingers, as do the associated assumptions of its unity and capacity to be known.

The aim of this chapter is to introduce some of the most influential perspectives in the study of the city and from this consideration to point to the need to understand cities as being simultaneously material and conceptual. It does this first by tracing key foundational ideas, including those of the Chicago School of Urban Sociology and the Marxism of Manuel Castells, David Harvey and Henri Lefebvre. The chapter also highlights the importance of methodology to the study of the city. What is evident from the discussion of this chapter is that until very recently and irrespective of theoretical orientation, urban studies has attempted to explain the city and urban life with reference to overarching and universal concepts and assumptions. Cities were seen as limited and knowable, and as producing cultures and ways of life that were predictable. It is now accepted, however, that such totalizing explanations are unsustainable. Not only are cities diverse and unpredictable, but so too are the cultures that form within urban space. Explanations of urban processes must take account of the networks and circuits that link different cities as well as different spaces within the same city. They must also be open to explanations forged at the micro level of the lived and the everyday, and so a key task of this chapter is to point to approaches that make this possible.

## Conceptualizing the city

Fundamental to the task of building social science knowledge about cities and urban life is the compilation (and utilization) of a theoretical language – a toolkit of concepts and categories which provides the frames, themes and metaphors required to reveal and explain urban trends and complexity. Concepts (and the urban processes and phenomena they interrogate and construct) are contested, interlocking and located. They are also incomplete, often ideological and deeply political. Concepts draw attention to the particular and provide entry points into a subject matter. If, however, they are engaged uncritically, in isolation, or as part of an oppositional binary, they can constrain and close off alternative ways of seeing and understanding. The city is itself a concept at the same time as being understood with reference to concepts, which means there is no one definitive set of explanations and no one definitive object that is 'the city'. Cities are the hard physical spaces of built infrastructure, architecture and planning as well as the soft spaces of representation, imagination and everyday life – simultaneously material, imagined and lived (Soja 1996). They are constructed through discourse, theory and use as well as at the interface of nature and culture.

The study of the city has a long history in sociology. Indeed, the development of the discipline is entwined with the growth of the modern industrial city, and many foundational sociologists, including Karl Marx, Max Weber, Émile Durkheim and Georg Simmel, all in some way engaged with the problem/issue of the city. For Simmel, the city – or 'metropolis', as he called it – was 'not a spatial entity with sociological consequences, but a sociological entity that is formed spatially' (Frisby 2007: 248). Weber (1958/1921) also analysed the city as a distinct form of social organization, framing it in terms of an 'ideal-type' (which made possible comparisons between cities/forms of urbanism) and emphasizing the role of economic activity, religious and legal institutions and political organization in cities and urban life. Importantly, for Weber, physical size was not a determinant of city status, at least not sociologically; rather, what mattered, in his view, were social institutions and the existence of particular forms of association.

During the twentieth century a sub-discipline of sociology emerged that was specifically concerned with the study of the city (see Savage and Warde 1993). Central considerations for urban sociologists include probing the relationship between the city and society, understanding the nature of urbanism, and examining the role of the state in processes of urban development and the allocation of urban resources. Urban sociologists have also examined the part played by the city in producing or supporting structures of social inequality, most notably those associated with class, gender, race and ethnicity, while some have pondered the nature and indeed very existence of a specific urban object of study. Urban sociology is anything but a unified field of inquiry. Rather, urban sociologists utilize, and engage with, a range of oft-competing theoretical and methodological approaches, many of which come from outside the discipline as part of the broader interdisciplinary field of urban studies. And with this variety has come the development of a raft of concepts and ways of seeing and explaining cities and urban society. For instance, some conceptualize the city as being a system comprised of interdependent networks and components, while others argue that the forces of capitalism have created cities that are sites of inequality and function to protect capitalism, private property and the accumulation of wealth – to highlight but two broad approaches.

The concern of many of the early urban sociologists was to develop a conceptual framework that was capable of explaining *all* cities and *all* urban processes, irrespective of their different histories, cultures and geographies. This goal was the urban sociological equivalent of seeking to formulate a 'theory of everything'. Of course, the focus of urban sociology was very much not only on 'Western' cities, but specifically those of the global North, and, as with sociology more generally, the concepts and theories developed were embedded in the intellectual context of this 'global metropole' (Connell 2010: vii). Most influential initially was the Chicago School of Urban Sociology, which was at its most active between 1915 and 1945, but dominated urban thinking until all but the last few decades of the twentieth century. The Chicago School sociologists, who used their home city as their 'laboratory', had two main concerns: to trace the patterns and processes of urbanization, including identifying their core characteristics, and to ascertain a uniform urban culture or 'way of life' and the social and spatial factors that produced it (Wirth 1995). And a coherent conceptualization of the city was pivotal. For instance, Louis Wirth (1995: 80), who was one of the most influential members of the Chicago School, explains that '[i]t is only insofar as the sociologist has a clear conceptualization of the city as a social entity and a workable theory of urbanism that he can hope to develop a unified body of reliable knowledge. . . .'

The city, for the Chicago School, was an ecological system or unity that adapted systematically and predictably in response to changes in population, demography and the physical environment. This was a 'characterization of the urban subject' which, according to Sharon Zukin (1980: 576), 'laid the basis for certain commonly accepted conceptualizations' of the city and urban life. It had a number of key dimensions. First, the Chicago School believed that, as with biological or ecological entities, urbanization and urban change followed predetermined patterns which were observable and, thus, predictable. Second, they regarded urbanization and a range of associated technological, social and cultural processes as being inextricably linked to modernization. Third, Chicago School accounts of the 'subjective factors' which shape urban morphology, including explanations of neighbourhood concentrations of particular ethnic groups, focused either on the personal preferences of residents, such as those associated with taste and social status, or on 'rationality or efficiency', whereby urban 'space seemed to reflect the characteristics of its inhabitants' (Zukin 1980: 576). Fourth, according to the sociologists of the Chicago School, the urban environment caused or amplified negative individual and social circumstances, such as crime and deviance. Finally, the role of the state was never questioned in Chicago School conceptualizations of cities, urbanization and urbanism, and if it was considered at all, it was assumed not to play any role beyond functioning to support urban and social 'needs'.

According to Wirth (1995), a city can be defined with reference to three interconnected variables: size, density and heterogeneity. The more of each of these variables a city has, the more urban that city is, while a change in any one, such as a decrease in population density, will lead to a change in the urban character of the city. In this respect, the city and urbanism are defined against their 'other' – the rural and rural life – creating a dualism that continues to permeate much urban thought (Stevenson 2003). The Chicago School also held the view that empirical research is required in order really to know the city and urban culture. As a result, not only did the Chicago School establish the conceptual parameters of a sociological understanding of the city that was hegemonic for most of the twentieth century, but they also developed a methodological approach to urban research that is still influential. Specifically, and as discussed further below, the Chicago School pioneered applied urban research that involved (often in combination) participant observation and the use of official and other statistics to map the social profiles of cities and neighbourhoods.

It was not until the 1970s that the supremacy of the urban ecology perspective of the Chicago School was successfully challenged. This challenge came first from a Weberian-informed urban sociology concerned with urban managerialism and housing classes (Rex and Moore 1967), and then most effectively from the Marxist perspectives that emerged in the wake of the urban crises of the mid- to late 1960s. What was crucial to Marxists was that Chicago School-inspired urban sociology had not only failed to predict the urban unrest, but that it also lacked the conceptual tools needed to explain it. The result was an intellectual crisis that went to the core of the sub-discipline. As Zukin (1980: 577) puts it, '[A] basic failure of conceptualization had led to almost total intellectual paralysis.' The critical approaches that developed in the explanatory vacuum created by the failure of urban ecology came initially to be known as the 'new urban sociology'.

## Urban sociology rethought

The new urban sociology had a number of core concerns which underpinned the conceptualization of cities and urban life. In particular, researchers saw the city in terms of conflict rather than consensus, and highlighted the significance of capitalist accumulation and class struggle to the processes of urban development and resource allocation. A strand of the new urban sociology emphasized the role of social relations, including gender, class and race, in shaping urban form.

Others regarded cultural meaning, imagination and the symbolic as important aspects of the development and experience of urban space. The significance of macro, global processes operating in combination with those of the national and the local was also highlighted, as was the role played by all levels of the state in managing urban space and urban populations to support capitalism. Finally, not only did the new urban sociology challenge the conceptual basis of the sub-discipline, but it also questioned its very object of analysis – the nature and existence of a set of social processes that were specifically urban rather than features more broadly of the social structure. In addition, although labelled 'sociology', this new field quickly emerged as interdisciplinary, with key insights coming from disciplines other than sociology, in particular geography. Considered together, these approaches formed a broadly 'sociospatial model' of explanation (Gottdiener and Hutchison 2006: 368) that stressed the importance of structures and connections. What was significant was the linking of urbanization to larger processes of industrial capitalism, effectively assigning urban ecology to the history of sociological thought.

In her tracing of the intellectual terrain of the new urban sociology, Zukin (1980: 582) suggests that two conceptualizations of the urban subject/object came to dominate the field: one that regarded the urban as 'the localization of social forces' and another that viewed it as 'the conduit of capital and control'. Zukin goes on to explain that both conceptualizations 'inspired a particular "wing" of the new urban sociology' that roughly divided along national lines. On the one hand were those French Marxists who were interested in the city as localization and to this end examined 'questions of how space is used in the process of social reproduction' – concerns such as social segregation and the inequitable distribution of urban resources were important to the French. American urban studies, on the other hand, was more interested in examining 'cities as conduits of capital investment and labor discipline' (Zukin 1980: 582). Key concerns for these urbanists included 'the growth and decline of particular urban areas, locational shift of economic enterprises and population, and the role of construction and real estate in the economy' (Zukin 1980: 582).

One of the most influential theorists in the French new urban sociology tradition was the Althusserian Marxist Manuel Castells, who, in examining the social movements and urban unrest of the late 1960s, set out to develop a systematic understanding of the urban processes of capitalism. In particular, Castells (1972) was concerned to assert the scientific basis of urban sociology and to identify the function of capitalism that was specific to the city and, therefore, the object of study of urban sociology. He concluded that it was consumption or, more accurately, 'collective consumption' that was functionally unique to the city and thus should be the object/subject of the sub-discipline. By collective consumption, Castells (1972: 75) meant services such as health, education, transport and town planning, the 'organization and management' of which 'cannot be other than collective given the nature and size of the problems'. Castells went on to argue that the provision (or lack) of collective services and resources was frequently a source of tension and could under certain circumstances lead to urban protest and unrest. He also argued that at the core of this unrest was the failure of the state to manage effectively both the distribution of urban resources and any resulting crises. In other words, for Castells the urban crisis was in effect one of collective consumption and the failure of urban governance/management. From this conceptualization, he went on to suggest that urban struggles over collective consumption had the potential to connect with working-class movements in ways that could result in the overthrow of capitalism. 'The city' for the Castells of *The Urban Question*, therefore, was the city of industrial capitalism and the capitalist state, 'urbanism' was the culture of this city, and 'urbanization . . . the integration of all remote regions into the capitalist world system' (Zukin 1980: 583).

Contrasting with the structural Marxism of Castells are the views of urban geographer David Harvey (1973, 1982), who is one of the most high-profile theorists in the American Marxist tradition of urban studies. Where Castells saw urban crises in terms of consumption, Harvey explained them in terms of a crisis of capital accumulation. In this, he was greatly influenced by Henri Lefebvre's (2003a/1970) argument that the entwined processes of urbanization and advanced capitalism have created a secondary circuit of capital – real estate investment – that is emerging to be more influential than the primary industrial circuit of capital. According to Harvey, over-investment in the manufacturing sector of the economy (the 'primary circuit' of capital) results in falling rates of profits and leads to the switching of investment capital from the primary to the built or second circuit of capital. For Harvey, it is these crises of accumulation that drive urban change and urbanization under capitalism. Where Harvey regarded this process as a 'cyclical' one 'of expansion and contraction synchronized with the pattern of capitalist growth and crisis' (Kipfer et al. 2008a: 7), Lefebvre (2003a/1970: 1) proposed that society was becoming 'completely urbanized' and proffered the idea of an 'urban revolution' and the possibility that urbanization was now the context for industrial capitalism: '[B]y "urban revolution" I refer to the transformations that affect contemporary society, ranging from the period when questions of growth and industrialization predominate (models, plans, programs) to the period when the urban problematic becomes predominant, when the search for solutions and modalities unique to urban society are foremost' (Lefebvre 2003a/1970: 5).

Lefebvre saw the survival of capitalism as being entwined with the processes of urbanization. Stefan Kipfer et al. (2008b: 290) point out that 'Lefebvre's hypothesis about complete urbanization was meant to apply to the world as a whole. The urban as a level of social reality is thus subject to analysis at multiple scales: the scale of metropolitan regions, national urban systems, and transnational, potentially global urban networks and strategies.' Although offering different sets of explanations, Marxist urban sociologists and geographers, nevertheless, shared a conceptualization of the city in terms of capitalist forces and generalizable principles. Thus, no matter the framework, the rhythms of cities, city building and capitalist accumulation are seen as entwined.

The critical approach of the new urban sociology continues to be influential in urban studies, and the key insights that were developed initially in response to the urban crises of the 1960s and then to the subsequent epistemological and ideological crises of the sub-discipline have remained instructive. They have again proved important as researchers seek to explain the urban dimensions of both the global financial crisis that commenced in the United States in 2007–8 and, more recently, the riots that occurred in many English cities in August 2011. Castells has moved away from his early work on the city, but it may well be timely to reflect on whether his political economy could contribute to understandings of such contemporary urban crises. In recent years an increasing number of urban researchers have come to be interested not just in the 'big' processes of urbanization, industrialization, urban protest and structural inequality but also in the everyday, lived aspects of cities, with several sophisticated analyses seeking to understand the city at both its macro and micro levels. To this end, many have looked to disciplines including, for instance, cultural studies for the theoretical tools to examine the city as a 'signifying object' and to understand the structures of meaning that underpin individual and collective relationships with, and within, cities and urban space (Stevenson 2003). Indeed, following cultural theorists such as Michel de Certeau (1988/1980), the necessity to understand the city as it is lived and imagined has become increasingly obvious. De Certeau contrasts the rational 'concept city' of the planner, architect and urban bureaucrat with the lived (and often subversive) city of everyday life and direct experience. He is interested, in particular, in the claiming and interpreting of cityspace that occurs through the act of walking or moving through space – what he terms the 'tactics of everyday life'.

De Certeau's focus is on the ways in which the everyday activities of the less powerful can subvert dominant social ideologies and power relations, but it is important to acknowledge that these micro rhythms and circuits emerge in the context of broader circuits of capital and rhythms of capital accumulation. This is a theme and set of relationships which feature in the increasingly influential work of Lefebvre, who was of the view that just as the macro cannot be read from the micro, the micro cannot be 'grasp[ed] . . . via the macro' (Lefebvre 2008a/1961: 140). The relationship between the two is complex, with the micro being positioned as 'the living root of the social' at the same time as the macro 'encompasses' the micro without determining it (Lefebvre 2008a/1961: 141). As Lefebvre (1991/1974: 412) further explains: 'Space's hegemony does not operate solely on the "micro" level, effecting the arrangements of surfaces in a supermarket, for instance, or in a "neighbourhood" of housing-units; nor does it apply only on the "macro" level, as though it were responsible merely for the ordering of "flows" within nations of continents.' It is his focus on the micro and the macro that makes Lefebvre's work and conceptual approach so useful to contemporary urban studies as it seeks to understand the symbolic and everyday aspects of urban  life without slipping into relativism at the same time as considering the bigger structural processes and relations that shape economies, societies and urban space.

## Complexity and the rhythms of everyday life

Lefebvre sought consistently throughout his intellectual career 'to raise questions about the conceptualization of the city, the rights of its citizens and articulation of time, space and the everyday' (Kofman and Lebas 2003: 6). Significantly too, Lefebvre's entwined concerns with the processes of urbanization, the production of space and the structure of everyday urban life led him to contemplate the importance of rhythms and the circulation of capital, meanings and ideas in urban space, as well as of 'moments', which are those ephemeral, transitory 'sensations (of delight, surrender, disgust, surprise, horror, or outrage) which were somehow revelatory of the totality of possibilities contained in daily existence' (Harvey 1991: 429). As one of the first sociologists to examine cities and space at different levels, Lefebvre explored both the liberating potential of everyday life and the nature and consequences of the political struggle over the production of urban space. This task was a complex and multifaceted one prosecuted across a substantial body of work. Although Lefebvre's work, unlike that of Castells, which was published in translation in the 1970s, did not become widely known in the English-speaking world until the 1990s, many of his ideas had been introduced by others before then, including most notably by David Harvey (1973) and Mark Gottdiener (1985), while a number of central concerns in Castells' urban sociology, particularly his arguments regarding the appropriate object of urban sociological analysis (discussed above), were proffered directly in response to the interventions of Lefebvre.

Importantly, in Lefebvre's view, it is the urban, conceptualized as an intervening space or 'level' between the private or everyday and the global realm of markets and institutions, that mediates the micro and macro levels of social reality. A triad comprising the 'global, the urban and the everyday' is a crucial aspect of this framework. Indeed, conceptual triads are important and recurring features of Lefebvre's work. For instance, central to his formulation of the production of space is a triad comprising: the 'perceived' space of material spatial practice; the 'conceived' or 'conceptualized' space of representation, particularly of language and thought; and lived-representational space that 'tend[s] towards more or less coherent systems of non-verbal symbols and signs' (Lefebvre 1991/1974: 38–9). Lefebvre's (2010/1992: 12) triadic formulations '[link] three terms that it leaves distinct, without fusing them in a *synthesis* . . .'. Thus the city is simultaneously material, imagined and lived, and these aspects can each be analysed separately and as 'mutually implicating principles' (Beck 2002: 17). This approach, Lefebvre contends, establishes a framework for explaining social and cultural change whilst at the same time creating the conceptual space for serendipity and possibility. Kofman and Lebas (2003: 9) suggest that this triadic analysis of space moves from the 'abstract to the concrete, from theory to reality', and it is also historical as well as conceptual (Elden 2010: ix). So, fused with a threefold formulation for the production of space is an historical analysis focused on what Lefebvre terms the 'abstract', 'relative', 'concrete' and 'absolute' dimensions of space. In Lefebvre's conceptualization, space is not a neutral container for action but deeply enmeshed in everyday social relations and their reproduction, and the relations of production and their reproduction (Schmid 2008: 41).

Lefebvre (2003a/1970) asserts possibilities and 'tendencies', intersections, simultaneity and relationships, not causation and primacy. The important point here, though, is that the influence of urbanization on industrialization (and vice versa) cannot uncritically be assumed – they are entwined elements of the productive trialectic of space. A significant aspect of Lefebvre's sociology is the concept of everyday life, which, as explained above, he conceptualizes in terms of its interrelationship with the global/general and the mediating urban. Everyday life is the level of experience that is centred on lived space and the household, rather than the workplace. It is the time and space that falls outside the realm of (paid) work and can be mundane and repetitive as well as fulfilling and creative. Everyday life is a productive interrelated zone of temporal and historical contradictions and dynamic tensions (Lefebvre and Régulier 2010/1992: 73). Kofman and Lebas (2003: 48) suggest that '[t]he everyday is the weaving of cyclical and linear time and of moments, while the urban is duration and passage. . . . [T]he right to the city includes the struggle for the appropriation of lived time.' This is an observation that goes to the heart of the struggle over the resources of the city and tensions focused on the city and city life, the suburbs and suburban life – the urban core and the marginal (and marginalized) periphery.

The notion of rhythms is a central element of this understanding of everyday life as well as part of Lefebvre's project for thinking about the simultaneity of space and time (Elden 2010: ix). Understanding everyday urban life through rhythms is not simply about tracking movement or even mobility through space, although clearly these are important. It is also about stasis and 'moments'. Although unfinished at the time of his death, Lefebvre's work on rhythmanalysis nevertheless provides a fascinating starting point for exploring 'relationships between different forms of movement and spatial arrangements, between durations and moments' (Highmore 2005: 9). City rhythms also relate to those extended temporal perspectives, such as *re*structuring, *re*building and *re*generation, as well as to the everyday rhythms that are lived and experienced in the homes and on the streets of the metropolis. As Ash Amin and Nigel Thrift (2008: 17) explain, 'The rhythms of the city are the coordinates through which inhabitants and visitors frame and order the urban experience. . . . [T]he city is often known and negotiated through these rhythms and their accompanying ordering devices (traffic rules, telephone conventions, opening times, noise control codes).' The proposition that cites and urban life are formed through the confluence of rhythms relates quite strikingly to urban temporalities, including, notably, 'day', 'night', 'morning', 'afternoon', 'evening', 'dawn' and 'dusk'. Although in Lefebvre's schema the rhythms of nature are fundamental to preindustrial daily life, they, nevertheless, remain central to the processes shaping the experience and spatiality of everyday life in the contemporary city. Seasonality, both in the formal guises of summer, winter, autumn and spring and informally through routine variances in the weather and the presence/absence/duration of sunlight, is an important element of the urban rhythmic, which shapes and describes not only the rhythms of the calendar year but also the experience of the micro intersections of time and space – 'summer nights', for instance, are very different both imaginatively and experientially from 'winter nights'. Urban economic activity is also subject to the rhythms of temporality and seasonality, with work, tourism, leisure and consumption being most evidently affected; but the weather conditions associated with the seasons can also profoundly shape transportation and trade in many parts of the world, and it is not uncommon for major airports to have night-time flight curfews. At their most simplistic, temporality and seasonality are the contexts or cloaks for urban life and social action, but more significantly they also structure and give shape to cities, urbanism and the urban imaginary.

## Theory, method, knowledge

It is simply not possible to understand the city or the concepts used to explain it without some appreciation of the methodologies of urban studies, in particular of the various intellectual traditions that have informed different approaches to researching cities and the way in which methodologies shape knowledge of the urban. For instance, Lefebvre's theorization of space, time and everyday life was embedded in a specific methodological approach involving, in particular, 'dialectical triads' (discussed above) which link theory and practice, as well as what he terms the method of 'regression and progression', which was observation combined with comparative and historical analyses (Lefebvre 1991/1974: 65–7). Kofman and Lebas (2003: 9) explain that regression 'combines genealogical (returning to the emergence of a concept and exploring its concrete affiliations, detours and associations) and historico-genetic procedures (abstract and total, linked to the general history of society and philosophy). Progression refers to the opposite move, that of beginning with the present and evaluating what is possible and impossible in the future.'

As discussed above, the Chicago School made the first systematic attempt to frame a specific methodological approach to the study of the city. The Chicago sociologists set out to identify the 'natural areas' of the city and then either 'map' the social profiles of these areas or, having identified a natural area, perhaps undertake an in-depth analysis of everyday life there. Researchers employed the methods of quantitative statistical analysis and/or qualitative participant observation. One outcome of their dual approach to studying the city was to foster the development of two rather discrete methodological traditions within urban sociology. The first of these traditions involved the 'ecological mapping' of whole cities and individual neighbourhoods, whereby census and other official statistics were used to produce locality profiles. From these statistics, researchers could chart the degree of residential homogeneity, diversity, social disorganization, the concentration of different ethnic, racial or social groups, and the distribution of social 'pathologies' and 'deviant behaviour', such as divorce, delinquency, mental illness, criminal activity and non-nuclear families, all of which Chicago School sociologists believed were causally related to the morphology of the city.

The second part of the urban research agenda developed by members of the Chicago School did not necessarily involve ecological mapping, although these data were often used as a starting point. Rather, the Chicago theorists advocated applying the ethnographic technique of participant observation to the study of urban life. In fact, one of the School's founders, Robert Park, reportedly advised his students of the need to 'get the seat of your pants dirty in real research' (quoted in Kasinitz 1995: 17). The ethnographic method of urban research that Park advocated required researchers to immerse themselves so thoroughly in the everyday life of the group being studied that the subtle and complex rules, values, norms and cultural practices of the group would be exposed. The result was a proliferation of detailed in-depth studies of a diverse range of urban subcultures and compelling descriptive accounts of the rich tapestry of life in the 'natural areas' first of Chicago, then, as the influence of the Chicago School spread, of cities around the world. The focus of research frequently was on the lives and social relations of those regarded as being on the margins of society – such as gangs (Thrasher 1927) or transients (Anderson 1923) – or on life in the urban ghettoes (Wirth 1927, 1928) and the so-called 'slum areas' of the city (Zorbaugh 1929). The ethnographies of the Chicago School were also influential in prompting the development of the 'community studies' tradition of sociology, which often involves in-depth analyses of life in small towns. Such ethnographies are so rich in descriptive detail that some have called them the sociological equivalent of the novel (Bell and Newby 1982).

Although looking for trends and patterns and advocating generalizable explanations of urban life, the work of the Chicago School also led to an acknowledgement of the diversity of urban cultures and the need to get in touch with them. As a result, and perhaps somewhat ironically given the Chicago School's tendency to generalize, detailed ethnographies of life in different parts of the city and in rural communities to some extent undermined a belief in the existence of a uniform urban experience or way of being (urbanism) by highlighting the diversity and complexity of the urban. Ethnographic research also provided evidence that people living in areas that to outsiders may look dysfunctional or boring (for instance, slums and homogeneous residential neighbourhoods) might actually enjoy positive interactions and everyday social relations. The classic work here is that of the British researchers Michael Young and Peter Willmott (1962), who conducted in-depth research over two years in Bethnal Green in East London and found that the working-class residents identified strongly with their neighbourhoods and had extremely close ties with their neighbours, many of whom were relatives.

According to Zukin (1980), the two 'wings' of the 'new' Marxist urban sociology that emerged in France and the United States in the 1960s and 1970s (discussed above) differed methodologically as well as in their research concerns. As she explains: 'The French studies . . . often chose an analysis which considers the city as a system of social action, but the American studies view the city as it functions within a larger system' (Zukin 1980: 582). She goes on to argue that this difference was shaped largely by researchers' observations of their own societies:

> For the Americans, this includes the presence of many large metropolitan agglomerations, marked changes in the pattern of regional dominance, an institutional history of urban (and suburban) autonomy in certain spheres of action, and the recent succession of urban and financial crises. For their part, the French must deal with a highly centralized, Paris-dominated economy, society, and culture; state-capitalized implantations of new regional centers; a more systematic penetration by international capital; and, due to national rather than local financing of social welfare expenditures, the absence of those contradictions which take the form of municipal fiscal crisis. (Zukin 1980: 582-3)

It was not only Marxist urban sociology, however, that was embedded in specific national, urban and cultural contexts, but urban studies more broadly and the dominant methodologies and explanatory frames of social science. Dominant perspectives are outcomes of having been shaped in the 'rich capital-exporting countries of Europe and North America – the global metropole' (Connell 2010: vii). Until relatively recently, explanations of cities and urban life around the world drew on frameworks developed in this physical and intellectual space and were grounded in conceptualizations of metropolitan modernity and 'located', both in reality and metaphorically, in the cities and the theoretical spaces of the global North. Little thought was given to the appropriateness (or adequacy) of these ways of seeing or to the consequences of devaluing knowledge, experience and perspectives formed outside the 'North' and with reference to cities that had developed through different processes and sets of social relations.

It is important to note that as part of a suite of qualitative and quantitative methods, observations at both the macro (structures, institutions and processes) and the micro (everyday life, lived cultures and rhythms) levels have been central to urban sociology in all its theoretical guises from the beginning of the sub-discipline. Urban sociology thus shares its methodological character and tensions with the broader discipline of sociology as it seeks to 'obtain organized knowledge of social reality' (Schutz 2004: 211). More recently, urban analysts have added the method of semiotics and the interpretation of urban texts to their methodological toolkits, and the study of a multiplicity of texts, both written and spatial, has provided valuable insights and deepened understandings of the dynamics of cities and city life.

Through combinations of theory, method, empirical interest and (intellectual and spatial) location, different cities and diverse, oft-competing, insights into the same city come into view. It is no longer expected that a theory of everything is possible or even desirable and it is now generally accepted that cities and urban life need to be examined at a number of levels and in terms of a range of conceptual and historical moments. These understandings inform the approach taken in this book, the overarching objective of which is to take the concept of the city and, with reference to an array of urban theories, examine how it has been understood, explained and experienced in a range of contexts. The inherent complexity of 'the city' means it is not possible to capture its diversity, scope and contradictions within a single conceptual frame or, indeed, a single book. Moreover, analyses of the city increasingly deploy metaphors – such as 'fluid city' (Dovey 2005), 'creative city' (Landry 2002), 'fantasy city' (Hannigan 1998), to name but three at random – as entry points into what is a multifaceted and disjointed subject matter, which is the approach adopted here. So in this spirit, and under the heading of 'material city', the next chapter explores different aspects of the relationship between capitalism and the contemporary city through a consideration of the themes of neoliberalism, industrialization, gentrification, ghettoization and the urbanization of contemporary China.

# 2

# Material City

## Economies and Inequalities

Modern urban settlements often incorporate the sites of traditional cities, and may look as though they have merely
grown out of them. In fact, modern urbanism is ordered
according to quite different principles from those which set
off the pre-modern city from the countryside in prior periods.
Giddens 1990: 6

## Introduction

In early 2007 the first signs emerged in the United States of
what quickly unfolded to be a global financial crisis of such
magnitude that by mid-2008 many nations were in recession.
Cities – house prices and mortgages – were central to this
crisis not only as the financial spaces that fractured to trigger
the economic meltdown, but also as the physical sites and
symbols of decline and despair, the visible evidence of breakdown and failure. The financial crisis revealed much about
the scope and texture of contemporary capitalism as well as
the interconnectedness of cities and nations and the consequences of their enmeshment in a global economic system
that is built on financial capital and demands continued
growth. As flagged by Anthony Giddens in the passage
quoted above, and explained in the previous chapter, the
processes of contemporary urbanization are driven substan-

tially by the imperative of capitalism – in particular, by the requirement to attract investment, maximize profit and absorb capital. These priorities, and the processes and principles they inform, are very different from those which prompted the development of the 'pre-modern city', and, in turn, they shape distinctive spatial forms and urban cultures. While it is unsustainable to speak of a single 'capitalist city' (the 'cities of capitalism' being perhaps more accurate), it is certainly the case that capitalism, urbanization and urbanism are deeply entwined, and this is an entanglement that has become even more hegemonic since the 1980s. The goals of enticing capital investment in all its forms and fostering international trade were pivotal in the 1980s to the removal of a raft of regulations and protocols that had been put in place after the Second World War to protect economies and societies from the extremes of capitalism, but that had come to be considered by some as barriers to growth and the accumulation of capital. It was the consequences of such factors that converged to create the conditions for the economic and urban turmoil of 2007–8.

The starting point for this chapter is the relationship between capitalism and the city, which it probes through three interconnected lenses, beginning with a consideration of the rise of neoliberalism, which has been the economic context of urban development worldwide for three decades. Neoliberalism and the deregulation of global financial markets in the West also coincided with the opening up of the Chinese economy to foreign investment and trade, which has led to the emerging importance of China to the world economy. Central to this growth are the conjoint processes of urbanization and industrialization. Neoliberalism is also implicated in the increasing spatial division and fragmentation that is evident in cities around the world. Of significance is a deepening of the inequitable distribution of urban resources, which, although taking a number of forms, is perhaps most highly visible in residential segregation. The markers of affluence, including the colonization by the middle class of working-class neighbourhoods and former industrial sites, and the creation of commercial, residential and consumption spaces in city centres, have frequently been accompanied by the growth of underserviced zones and neighbourhoods elsewhere in the city. The 'planet of slums' (Davis 2004, 2006) and the planet of capital and prosperity coexist in the contemporary city. In this context, it is relevant that the processes of gentrification and ghettoization are occurring at the same time as the growth of underserviced slums and shantytowns are occurring simultaneously.

## Spaces of neoliberalism

From the early days of the discipline, sociologists have drawn attention to, and sought to explain, the built and social consequences of capitalism, including the evident geographies of inequality and deprivation that were an outcome of industrial capitalism. For instance, Marx's collaborator Friedrich Engels (1969/1892: 96) graphically details the squalid living conditions he observed in the slums of England's emerging industrial city of Manchester, declaring that 'in the working-men's dwellings . . . no cleanliness, no convenience, and consequently no comfortable family life is possible; . . . in such dwellings only a physically degenerate race robbed of all humanity, degraded, reduced morally and physically to bestiality, could feel comfortable and at home.' Similarly, the noted urban historian Lewis Mumford (1989/1961: 447) observed that '[i]ndustrialism, the main creative force of the nineteenth century, produced the most degraded urban environments the world had yet seen. . . .'

As discussed in Chapter 1, although differing in their concerns and approaches, Marxists all regard the capitalist relations of production as the motor for, and context of, contemporary urbanization, shaping the physical, social and cultural structure and organization of cities, as well as the conditions of urban life. The starting point in each case is the relationship between the ruling capitalist class (the bourgeoisie), which owns the means of production, and the workers or proletariat, upon whose labour power the capitalist system depends. Marxists argue that capitalism, as an economic and social system, and a ('antagonistic' and 'exploitative') relationship that exists between the two domi-

nant classes, is formed through the entwined and often contradictory circuits of production, exchange, consumption
and investment. Cities, as the sites of industry and thus of
work, are regarded as the spaces where the capitalist relations and forces of production coexist and class-based
 inequalities of wealth, opportunity, housing and amenity
flourish. Cities, therefore, are places of struggle and where,
according to this perspective, the conditions also exist for
overturning capitalism.

Following the Second World War and with the memory
of the Great Depression still fresh, Western governments put
in place a set of economic policy initiatives and international
agreements and protocols that were designed to set the
parameters for the operation of capitalism. Of particular
relevance was an international system of financial and trade
management known as Bretton Woods, and the influence of
the theories of the British economist John Maynard Keynes.
The overarching aim of the post-war Bretton Woods consensus was to avoid a repeat of the Depression of the 1930s,
and to this end governments took the view, first, that it was
necessary to initiate a range of national policies that would
maintain high levels of (male) employment, and, second, that
the establishment of a set of transnational agreements and
institutions was required to ensure that 'depressive forces'
were not 'transmitted through the international payments
and trading system' (Skidelsky 2010: 99). The 1944 Bretton
Woods agreement also set up a system of fixed exchange
rates which was backed by gold reserves, and the US dollar
became the reserve currency for the world – a move which
fused the global economy with that of the United States
(Harvey 1989a: 137). Established at this time were the International Monetary Fund (IMF), to oversee the global financial system, and the World Bank, to provide loans to
developing nations for capital programmes. According to
David Harvey (2007: 11), the resulting post-war policy and
economic organization

> is now usually referred to as 'embedded liberalism' to signal
> how market processes and entrepreneurial and corporate
> activities were surrounded by a web of social and political
> constraints and a regulatory environment that sometimes

restrained but in other instances led the way in economic and industrial strategy. State-led planning and in some instances state ownership of key sectors (coal, steel, automobiles) were not uncommon. . . .

This post-war period of expansionary government, managed global capitalism and growing international trade and finance was accompanied in many nations, notably the United States, by a major economic boom which created considerable personal, corporate and national wealth. This was also a time of significant urbanization, including mass-suburbanization, in many Western cities. Indeed, the suburban form became something of a marker of prosperity (see Chapter 3). The post-war period was also a time of large-scale public housing projects, and in many European cities this building frequently took the form of high-rise estates, which were regarded by many as representative of the optimism of the times (Stevenson 2003). From the late 1960s, however, significant changes in national and international economic circumstances led in the 1970s to a rupturing, first, of national prosperity and then of the post-war Bretton Woods agreement and the hegemony of Keynesianism. At the core of the crisis were rapid inflation and growing unemployment – which in combination come to be known as 'stagflation' (Harvey 2007; Skidelsky 2010). Harvey (2007) argues that a crisis of capital accumulation was a pivotal factor leading to the economic downturn of the 1970s. This time of economic decline was marked in many cities by dramatic spatial decline as capital withdrew and industries and businesses closed. Indeed, many cities, most notably New York, were almost bankrupt. It was the economic crisis of the late 1970s that created the political space for the rise in the 1980s of the economic and political doctrine of neoliberalism, which was a 'strategic political response to [a] sustained global recession' (Brenner and Theodore 2004: 2–3). Underpinned by the belief that economic freedom and, in particular, the system of private property is the prerequisite for other forms of freedom (Hayek 2005/1944), neoliberalism advocates small government, free markets and the rights of the individual. It is a view that emerged in direct opposition to the fiscal and monetary approaches that had been

hegemonic in non-communist countries from the end of the
Second World War. Pivotal, in Harvey's view, to the emergence of neoliberalism was the aim to re-establish the conditions necessary for capital accumulation and reinvestment in
the built environment. Where, however, the foundational
goal of the post-war economic approach was to protect jobs
and maintain full employment, the neoliberal agenda was
concerned with fighting inflation, which at times has been
achieved at the expense of jobs. Central to the neoliberal
approach is the deregulation of industry, finance and labour;
liberalization of trade and markets; winding back the welfare
state; and selling public enterprises and utilities. Neoliberalism is also associated with increasingly entrepreneurial
approaches to urban governance whereby the concern is not
the usual activities of the local state – the management and
provision of services, including the 'three Rs' of 'roads, rates
and rubbish' – but local economic development and attracting capital investment (Harvey 1989b; see also Chapter 7).
Cities, their development and reimaging, were at the epicen-
tre of this agenda.

Critical moments in the ascent of neoliberalism were the
election in the United Kingdom of the Conservative government of Margaret Thatcher in 1979 and then, a year later in
the United States, the election of the Republican President
Ronald Reagan. Under the leaderships of Thatcher and
Reagan and, in an effort to stimulate economic growth and
reduce inflation, 'markets were deregulated, taxes were
lowered, trade unions were bashed, and international institutions were emasculated' (Skidelsky 2010: 99). A new regime
of flexibility in labour, production and consumption emerged
along with new approaches to city building and governance.
With these emerging techniques and processes came an
increase in the power, autonomy and internationalization of
the banking and financial systems. Indeed, Harvey (1989b:
164) argues that under neoliberal conditions of 'flexible
accumulation' the financial system assumed a pivotal coordination role 'at the expense of the power of the nation
state to control capital flow and, hence, its own fiscal and
monetary policy'. In other words, nations and indeed cities
became vulnerable to shifts in the flow of global capital over
which they had no control. As Doreen Massey (2011) details,

for some cities the spatial, social and economic consequences of the vagaries of 'footloose capital' (Martin and Rogers 1995) were devastating, but for others, in particular London and New York, the financial sector became the foundation of their prosperity. The geographies of neoliberalism were uneven both within and between cities and nations.

The consequences of neoliberalism were thus profound, with Connell (2010: 153) being but one of many to observe that its 'advent' had effects that extended well beyond the economic. The neoliberal agenda came, if not to permeate, then at least to influence in some way most aspects of every-day life, including social relations, the production and circu-lation of knowledge, and the production and experience of cities and urban space. The gap between rich and poor widened and homelessness increased in the cities of many developed nations – including those cities doing best out of the new economic and political regime. In developing nations, neoliberal policies and approaches, such as those imposed through the operation of the World Bank, also had profound

[handwritten marginal note: Social experiences of neoliberalism]

2.1  Canary Wharf financial district, London, UK.

effects on city building, as Grant and Nijman (2006) explain with reference to the 'corporate geographies' of Accra, Ghana and Mumbai, India (also see Chapter 7 below). Even in communist China the economy has increasingly liberalized since 1978, when Deng Xiaoping commenced the process of moving the national economy from being one that was closed and centrally planned to being much more market-orientated and open to international trade and foreign investment. The result has been the creation of a hybrid economic system whereby neoliberalism operates in tandem with centralization to support China's increased involvement in the global economy.

Neoliberalism dominated economies, governance and city building almost unchallenged until the global financial crisis of 2007–8. The trigger for this predicament was the subprime mortgage crisis in the United States, which led to bank foreclosures on home loans in cities across the nation but most particularly in poorer urban areas. By the end of 2007, approaching two million people in the US had lost their homes. Harvey (2010: 1–2) explains that '[h]ousing values plummeted almost everywhere across the US and many households found themselves owing more on their houses than they were worth. This set in motion a downward spiral of foreclosures that depressed housing values even further.' The consequences did not end there – banks and other financial institutions either failed or were at risk of doing so, stock markets plunged (Gotham 2009) and banks stopped lending to each other, and even more people either lost their homes or could not sell them because of the collapse of housing markets in the United States, the United Kingdom and elsewhere. What had begun as a problem in the US housing finance sector, in part because of a failure of banking regulation, soon affected the economies of almost every country in the developed world. In Ireland, for instance (a country which had once been held up as creating an 'economic miracle' through deregulation, low taxes and relaxed financial controls), the consequences of the economic crisis were severe, with unemployment and inflation rising dramatically, major industries shutting down or being downsized, and the property market collapsing. Similarly, halted was the fledgeling 'renaissance' of many so-called rustbelt cities in the

United Kingdom and elsewhere that had commenced in the 1980s and 1990s in response to the challenges of deindustrialization.

In probing the causes of the global financial crisis, most commentators point to a coincidence of factors. For instance, up until the 1980s, loans such as home mortgages were held in commercial and savings banks, but with changes to government policy and global financial markets and practices resulting from deregulation and increased neoliberalism, lenders were able to repackage these loans and sell them on global securities markets – a process that is termed 'securitization' (Gotham 2009). The result in the US was an increase in the number of mortgages being given to people who did not have the capacity to service the loan and an associated inability on the part of lending institutions and regulators to manage what became systemic financial risk. Thus, as prominent political economist Robert Skidelsky (2010: 4) explains, 'a global inverted pyramid of household and bank debt was built on a narrow range of underlying assets – American house prices. When they started to fall, the debt balloon started to deflate.' This explanation pivots on the belief that 'loose monetary and fiscal policy enabled Americans to live beyond their means' (Skidelsky 2010: 4), which, in turn, created a situation where an oversupply of money in the system resulted in an unsustainable asset (housing) 'bubble' forming.

There is an alternative view of the causes of the financial crisis, however, which is also sketched by Skidelsky (2010), and this is one that, informed by Keynesianism, emphasizes the role of savings in creating the conditions for crisis and argues that the problem lay in there being a global excess of savings *vis-à-vis* investment, with the savings held in Asia outstripping investment in the United States – China, as US Secretary of State Hillary Clinton reportedly once said, had come to assume the role of global 'banker'. Interestingly, Skidelsky points out that both these explanations of the 2007 downturn mirror those mounted to explain the Depression of the 1930s, which, ultimately, led to the Bretton Woods agreement and the introduction of the post-war financial strategies to manage the investment/savings ratio so reviled by neoliberal economists and politicians.

The global crisis of financial capitalism not only differentially affected cities, but it also had national consequences that were uneven. For instance, as industrial production and financial investment were abandoning the cities of the North from the 1980s, these moved, in large part, to the cheaper labour markets of the developing economies, most notably China, where industrialization has sparked massive urbanization. Indeed, the conjoint processes of industrialization and urbanization (but this time in the nations of the South) as well as neoliberalism continue to reside at the centre of the contemporary global economy.

## On the edges of affluence

China emerged as global economic powerhouse not only by embracing many of the principles of neoliberalism, but also by taking advantage of the changes that were occurring at the time in Western economies and forms of regulation, including the transformation of international markets and the unravelling of Bretton Woods (Harvey 2007). Important to the process of marketization and industrialization in China and the reshaping of its cities was the devolution of a range of financial and economic responsibilities from the national to the local level, which, in turn, meant that cities and regions became the motors of industrial development, innovation and economic growth. Zhu Jieming (2004) explains that local Chinese states have come to operate as semi-autonomous economic interest groups that are strongly focused on local enterprises and are in fierce competition with other states and regions (both nationally and internationally) for investment capital. Thus the city is squarely at the centre of the Chinese marketization process and pivotal was the designation in the early 1980s of 'Special Economic Zones' (SEZs).

The central government of China selected four cities – Shenzhen, Shantou, Xiamen and Zhuhai – as SEZs which had the administrative autonomy to seek foreign investment and undertake a range of market reforms designed to link them to international trade and capital markets (Chen 2010).

They were thus at the forefront of market-orientated economic development and the opening up of the Chinese economy. In 1984, the Chinese government expanded the SEZs initiative to include fourteen 'open cities', or Economic and Technical Development Zones, which also had the authority to attract foreign investment and pursue an agenda of market-based economic development and international engagement. Where the SEZs were constructed from scratch, however, these open cities set out to use this special status as the trigger to revitalize their existing urban infrastructure. Shanghai was one such city, and it has quickly become a major hub for trade, finance and shipping, emerging to be one of the most important economic centres in China and indeed the world. Massive urban and infrastructure development, including spectacular architecture, has accompanied the city's renewal. For instance, 293 million square metres of old housing was demolished between 2001 and 2005 and 447,900 households were physically moved as part of a significant housing construction, redevelopment and relocation process (Gidley 2010).

In 2010, Shanghai hosted World Expo under the intriguing slogan of 'Better City, Better Life'. This event was promoted as a marker of Shanghai's modernization and global status as well as the impetus for redeveloping 5.28 square kilometres of riverside land, much of which had been the location of factories, warehouses and shipping facilities. The national capital, Beijing, which has also undergone massive urban and economic change since the 1980s (although not as a designated SEZ or 'open city'), similarly featured the hosting of a mega-event – the Olympic Games in 2008 – as an element of its urban transformation strategy and to announce the nation's emergence as a global power. Both the Expo and the Olympics involved substantial programmes of infrastructure building and urban clearances, including in the case of the Olympics constructing new subway lines, an airport terminal, new roads and sporting venues and a light railway (Rowe 2011, 2012).

Another key aspect of China's urban transformation has been the implementation of a range of policies designed to move the nation's housing stock from state ownership to greater private home ownership. The result, as Zhu (2004)

**2.2   Terminal 3 Beijing Airport, China, designed by Norman Foster.**

reports by way of example, was that by 2001, after a decade of housing market reform, over 70 per cent of the housing stock in Beijing was privately owned. Just how affordable to the majority of Chinese residents the new market-provided housing is remains an open question, and of course there has been scant attention given to the affective and cultural consequences of displacement or to the destruction of historical areas, including the *hutong*, the narrow streets and alleyways formed by traditional Chinese courtyard residences. Frequently, too, traditional buildings are destroyed only to be replaced by replicas. For instance, a traditional Chinese temple in Beijing was demolished in the process of developing the massive Olympic precinct and a new temple was built on the same site.

A consequence of the policy to nominate SEZs and open cities has, in the words of one commentator, been 'to unleash the power of an urban revolution that has transformed the Chinese city' (Chen 2010: 128). China and its city building has for some time now been absorbing much of the world's surplus capital. While industrialization is an important driver of urbanization in developing nations, natural population growth and the mass movement of people from rural areas to the cities are also important. This movement is occurring at an astonishing pace even in nations that are not industrializing or necessarily even experiencing economic growth. According to the urban commentator Doug Saunders (2010: 22), 'Each month, there are five million new city-dwellers created through migration or birth in Africa, Asia and the Middle East.' Of course, migration from the country to the city occurs across, as well as within, national borders.

The processes of urbanization occurring in the South share many features of the urbanization that occurred in Europe as a result of its industrial revolution, but in Mike Davis's (2004: 8–9) view it goes further: 'The dynamics of Third World urbanization both recapitulate and confound the precedents of nineteenth- and early twentieth-century Europe and North America. In China the greatest industrial revolution in history is the Archimedean lever shifting a population the size of Europe's from rural villages to smog-choked sky-climbing cities.' The outcome is not simply that the majority of the world's population will soon live in urban centres, but that a staggering proportion will live in the slums and shantytowns of the world's megacities and many will have little prospect of ever participating in the 'formal' urban economy or the civic life of the city.

Shantytowns are congested, their sanitation systems are overwhelmed, waterways are polluted, and the shelters (which pass for housing) are inadequate and often unsafe. Their growth is what Davis (2004) refers to as the 'urbanization of poverty'. In Mexico City, for instance, '60 per cent of its nearly 20 million inhabitants liv[e] in illegal and informal housing' (Burdett and Rode 2010: 10). Saunders (2010) labels as 'arrival cities' many of the spaces on the fringes of major cities that have become home to an ever-expanding ex-rural population. According to him (Saunders 2010: 3), these arrival cities (be they sprawling or compact) have the potential to foment waves/upheavals of both prosperity and unrest. They are not static or predictable, but places where populations and cultures are in flux, and while, in Saunders' view, this brings considerable risks to already-existing urban populations, it is at the same time a context that is alive with possibilities which, he argues, need to be acknowledged and nurtured by authorities. The space of rural–urban transition is as much a space of cultural, social and economic change as it is a physical environment. They can be places of production and creativity. Of course, as movement out of these so-called 'arrival cities' is not assured, ways of encouraging transition within the space need to be imagined and implemented by city authorities.

Saunders' somewhat idiosyncratic and possibly overly optimistic account is at its core a celebration of the city and urban life and an acknowledgement of the potential of both. He is not alone in arguing that there is a correlation between the level of urbanization of a nation and its prosperity, including the standard of living and quality of life of residents. In 'wealthy nations', such as Japan, Australia and those of North America and Western Europe, between 72 and 95 per cent of the population lives in cities, whereas in Africa and Asia the percentage is 38 and 41, respectively. Saunders argues that the increased wealth of the West is directly connected to its high levels of urbanization and the associated decline in the proportion of the population living in rural areas.

The high-profile American economist Edward Glaeser (2011) is another who asserts the link between cities and prosperity, both cultural and economic. He puts forward an uncompromising argument in favour of cities and in particular of high-density urban life. Frequently functionalist – 'poverty often shows that a city is functioning well' (Glaeser 2011: 257) – and idealistic, his book *Triumph of the City* nevertheless maps a fascinating assessment of urbanism. Put simply, Glaeser argues that principally because of their density, cities facilitate face-to-face interaction, are places of innovation, attract people of talent, encourage competition and entrepreneurialism, and nurture a range of social and economic opportunities that do not emerge in low-density environments. Countries that urbanize, he contends, tend to be more productive and, hence, richer than those that do not. But the urbanization he advocates is not focused on the arrival edges of the city, nor does it have much in common with the influential 'city-as-village' perspective of prominent pro-urbanists such as Jane Jacobs (1993/1961), who, whilst

acknowledging that the 'diverse economic and social structures' of cities are 'engines of growth' (Florida 2009: np),
stressed the human scale of the city, its streetscapes and
neighbourhoods – what some would call its non-cityness
(Stevenson 2003). Nor does Glaeser's city take the form of
the low-rise European city or involve ever-expanding tracts
of suburbia. Rather, his is unapologetically a 'city-as-city'
view, which celebrates high-rise, high-density urban landscapes and lifestyles. In advocating the generative power of
the dense and compact city, Glaeser further argues that they
are actually less resource-intensive and thus more environmentally sustainable than low-density, car-dependent (and
hence carbon-producing) environments, notably the suburbs
(also see Chapter 3). In this respect, he is sharply critical of
the range of government housing and transportation policies
implemented over many decades in the United States and
elsewhere that have aggressively fostered what to his mind
are unsustainable levels of suburban growth.

Glaeser is one in a long line of urban theorists to probe
the issue of urban density and the role it plays in shaping
economies and societies – the early sociologists of the Chicago
School, notably Louis Wirth, placed density at the centre of
their conceptualizations of the city and urbanism, as did
Georg Simmel (see Chapter 5). Bruce Katz and Andy Altman
(2010: 96) also pick up this theme, claiming that 'hidden
beneath the story of sprawl and decentralization there is an
emerging narrative about the power and potential of cities
and urban places'. This narrative is one of density and economic and demographic change. As Katz and Altman (2010:
97) explain, 'the shift to an economy based on ideas and
innovation changes the value and function of density', not
only of building form and residential concentration, but also
the clustering of employment and services. In their assessment, building denser cities is also 'fiscally sound' when
compared with the suburban alternative, in part because
density reduces infrastructure costs. The reality, however, is
that few cities are becoming dense in their centres at the
expense of sprawl. Rather, both trends are occurring simultaneously in most major cities, either as a consequence of
policy and planning or through haphazard migration and
development. Lacking in most accounts of the benefits of

urban density, however, is any examination of the social consequences of high-density living for the urban poor. The examples that come readily to mind are the public housing tower blocks built in Europe in the 1950s and 1960s and which are now the sites of social breakdown and intergenerational disadvantage (Hall 1992). The high-density neighbourhoods of the poor frequently support very different social relations and conditions of everyday life than those found in high-density middle- and upper-income areas. Inequality and the uneven geography of wealth and poverty are key themes in this context – enclaves of advantage, ghettoes of disadvantage.

The idea of the ghetto has a long history as a concept in urban studies (Haynes and Hutchison 2008: 352), with Louis Wirth usually being credited with undertaking the first sociological analysis of the 'ghetto' in the 1920s. Wirth set out to examine how the Jewish population of Chicago was adjusting to urban life in America, and to this end he focused on the history and 'cultural life' of the ghetto in which they lived. For Wirth, the ghetto was a 'natural area' formed by the ecological processes of invasion, competition, accommodation and assimilation – the same processes that, he argues, shape the city as a whole. According to Wirth, the first generation of Jewish immigrants from Europe to Chicago had congregated initially in a specific zone of the city – forming a ghetto – but over time, as their economic, educational and social opportunities improved, many Jews moved out of the ghetto to other areas of the city. In Wirth's assessment, this was undesirable because the natural history of the Jews was one of outsider-hood, which was a status that made residential clustering both necessary and appropriate. It was, he argued, a key factor in building and maintaining cultural strength – an essential incubator of tradition and cultural practice. The Jews, according to Wirth (1927: 57), were 'a product of ghetto life', with Jewish culture and identity being significantly shaped through a history of living in ghettoes. Thus Wirth was concerned that residential assimilation and dispersal beyond the ghetto would have a negative effect on Jews' way of life, breaking down their culture and undermining a key source of collective identity. Although Wirth viewed the ghetto as a specifically 'Jewish institution', the term soon came to be used to refer to urban concentrations of all people from the same ethnic or racial background. In the United States the term 'ghetto' is also closely associated with African American neighbourhoods (Du Bois 1899; Haynes and Hutchison 2008), many of which are fractured by entrenched patterns and 'codes' of 'interpersonal violence and aggression' which sociologists argue are the outcomes of 'the lack of jobs that pay a living wage, limited basic public services . . . the stigma of race, the fallout from rampant drug use and drug trafficking, and the resulting alienation and absence of hope for the future' (Anderson 1999: 32).

Herbert Gans (2008: 353) draws a distinction between voluntary and involuntary urban segregation, suggesting that 'the ghetto is a place to which the subjects or victims of the involuntary segregation process are sent'. He explains that '[p]laces occupied by the voluntarily or self-segregated have generally been described not as ghettos but as enclaves. . . . "Mixed neighborhoods," which are shared by involuntarily and voluntarily segregated people, are thus ghettos for some and enclaves for others.' Gans goes on to argue that although ghettoization in the West is characterized by race and ethnicity, these are not its causes. Rather, for him it is class inequality and the economic structures and processes that produce extremes of wealth and poverty that are pivotal to the formation of ghettoes and, by extension, the establishment of enclaves.

The ghettoes of poverty and disadvantage frequently adjoin the enclaves of affluence and prosperity, a proximity and visibility which has become more pronounced under conditions of neoliberal urbanization and has led to a repositioning and increasing marginalization of the ghetto (and its residents) in contemporary urban narratives. David Wilson (2008: 211), taking a broader view, points to 'the rise of a new post-1990 regime of ghettoization that embodies the interplay of evolving economics, political formations, constructions of culture, and production of space'. Central here is an intersection between globalization and neoliberalism that requires cities to be economically competitive and thus includes competing globally for capital. Davis's (1990) searing account of Los Angeles as a city of urban and social division is an important illustration of the texture of residential segregation. Divisions are evident not only in the emergence of vastly different (and highly segregated) residential environments, but also in the widespread development of privately owned leisure, entertainment and retailing precincts, including the suburban shopping centres which are replacing the 'main street' as the principal shopping spaces of the middle and upper classes in many cities (see Chapter 7). Important, too, are the processes of gentrification whereby run-down, often working-class neighbourhoods, including many ghettoes and slums, come to be regarded by the middle class as attractive places in which to live. The result is the displacement of the poor and a reshaping of the geography of wealth and poverty.

## Gentrification and displacement

It was the British sociologist Ruth Glass who in 1964 coined the term 'gentrification' to describe the (then-emerging) trend of middle-class residents moving into traditional working-class areas and forcing the original (poorer) occupants to move out as local property values rose. American-based Marxist geographer Neil Smith (1982: 139) defines gentrification as 'the process by which working class residential neighborhoods are rehabilitated by middle class homebuyers, landlords, and professional developers'. Although displacement can be hard to measure or map, when low-income residents move out of an area in search of affordable housing, they frequently go to neighbourhoods located in the suburbs on the urban fringe. Conversely, it was often suburban life and its perceived homogeneity that the early gentrifiers were rejecting in favour of the residential diversity found in cheaper inner-city neighbourhoods. With gentrification comes the restoration of (often 'heritage') housing stock, the conversion of former warehouses or factory spaces into residences, and the establishment of middle-class retailing and consumption spaces. These factors combine to contribute to increasing both property values and the desirability of an area, which, in turn, results in an upsurge in the number of middle-class residents seeking to live there. Subsequent gen-

2.3  Former hospital now apartment complex, Sydney, Australia.

trifiers, as Fran Tonkiss (2005: 81) explains, are attracted not so much by 'social and economic diversity' and housing affordability, because these characteristics may well no longer be present, but by 'the effects of gentrification itself: renovated housing, new spaces of consumption and middle class residents'.

Gentrification thus is not a singular process; it is at once demographic, spatial, economic, social and cultural. It operates at the macro level of economic and political structures and practices as well as at the micro level of everyday urban cultures. Differing also between cities and nations, gentrification involves the simultaneous production of the material and symbolic dimensions of space. Mike Savage and Alan Warde (1993: 80) explain that there are a number of different (but not necessarily exclusive) academic explanations for gentrification. These approaches broadly fall into two categories: those that focus on 'supply' side factors, such as capital investment, and those concerned with 'demand' and the choices of residents. In other words, for some it is material factors, in particular class and the circulation of capital, that are important, while others emphasize the processes of consumption, culture and lifestyle. Many, of course, also acknowledge the importance of both investment and consumption to gentrification and argue that a comprehensive understanding of gentrification is one that engages with the dynamic interplay of supply and demand.

A highly influential account of the role of supply factors to gentrification is that of Neil Smith (1979, 1982, 1996), who drew on Harvey's work, in particular, to develop what he calls the 'rent gap hypothesis'. Smith asserts that it is changes in the nature of capital investment in the inner areas and not the consumption decisions of middle-class residents that lead to gentrification – 'Gentrification is a back-to-the-city movement all right, but a back-to-the-city movement by capital rather than people' (Smith 1996: 70). In Smith's view, urban neighbourhoods become run down because of a withdrawal of investment capital, but, over time, this lack of investment combines with the urban decline that it creates to present the conditions for new investment opportunities and, as a result, capital soon returns to the area. Put differently, disinvestment leads to urban decline, but at a certain point undercapitalization causes the 'rent gap [to grow] sufficiently large' (Smith 1996: 70) so as to make the neighbourhood ripe for redevelopment and hence reinvestment. The victims here, as Smith points out, are the residents living in these neighbourhoods before, during and after they have been abandoned by investors, but who become displaced by a reinvestment process focused on renovating or rebuilding the housing stock in ways that make it attractive to the middle class and hence increase its value.

The Canadian geographer David Ley (1980) is one who emphasizes not the role of capital investment in the processes of gentrification, but patterns of consumption, post-industrialism and what he terms the 'liberal ideology' of a new middle or cultural class comprised of professional, administrative and technical workers. With reference to research conducted in the city of Vancouver, Ley argues that a fraction of the new middle class was successful in setting the urban planning and development agenda in that city, which included mobilizing the discourse of the 'liveable city' to support the redevelopment and gentrification of a former inner-city industrial zone known as False Creek. Richard Florida's

(2003) exposition on the 'rise of the creative class' is also relevant (see Chapter 3). What Ley, Florida and others have also noted is the extent to which professional (often child-less) women and an increasing number of gays and lesbians are over-represented in the 'new' gentrifying class. In this context, Savage and Warde (1993: 85) suggest that '[t]he rise of gentrification is also the story of the rise of new forms of middle-class social groups, and thus shows how the forma-tion of particular urban spaces is intimately tied up with the development of social groups themselves.'

The arts and cultural industries also play a key role in gentrification, both informally, through the seemingly seren-dipitous presence of artists in run-down neighbourhoods, which, in turn, makes these places attractive to the 'new middle class', and more formally through the direct interven-tions of governments seeking to create arts and cultural precincts often in former industrial zones (see Chapter 3). Graeme Evans (2001), for instance, discusses the promotion by governments at all levels (including the transnational) of culture-led inner-city regeneration, which often involves building flagship cultural facilities or designated 'cultural precincts'. In her path-breaking account of the gentrification of 'downtown' Manhattan, Sharon Zukin (1989) details the importance of artists moving into the declining area in search of affordable studio space, which, in turn, made the neigh-bourhood appealing to the middle class.

According to Zukin, in little over a decade from the 1960s (and facilitated by changes to government regulations), many of the lofts of SoHo which were being vacated by light indus-try became occupied by artists. This was not a traditional working-class neighbourhood or ghetto being colonized, but a light manufacturing one that in deindustrializing had become ripe for readaptation. Zukin (1989: 6) describes the scale of the change that occurred in the neighbourhood: 'At the beginning of the 1960s, estimates of the number of artists living and working in lofts ranged between three thousand and five thousand. By the end of the seventies, it is possible over fifty thousand artists and non-artists were living in lofts that had been converted to residential use.' The presence of a high concentration of artists and related facilities, such as galleries, was thus instrumental in transforming SoHo into a 'cultural zone', making the area increasingly attractive to investors and middle- and upper-middle-class residents. As a result, rents began to rise and eventually the original artist-occupiers moved out in search of cheaper accommodation. A number of factors are noteworthy from this example. First, artists can and do play an important role in making an area desirable to the middle class and thus vulnerable to gentrification. Views differ on how best to interpret this role. For some commentators, artists are the 'storm-troopers of gentrification' (Evans 2001: 172), while others suggest that, rather than being 'storm-troopers', they are in effect the 'Trojan Horse for developers and "middle class" elites' (Montgomery 2008: 314). Second, artists move into low-rent areas because their incomes are low and rental properties in these areas are affordable. However, and this is the third point, while the presence of artists is important in making an area attractive to investors and gentrifiers, once this happens the artists are as susceptible to being displaced as are working-class residents in the traditional model of gentrification, to wit 'artists whose activities had created a desirable place to live [displace] themselves in doing so' (Worpole 1991: 148).

With gentrification also comes a rise in the urban service economy of lowly paid workers, including cleaners, wait staff, shop assistants and personal care workers, who under conditions of neoliberalism are frequently in precarious employment. Indeed, the consumption and lifestyle priorities of the creative new middle class to a very great extent depend on the labour of a marginalized workforce who frequently cannot afford to live in the gentrified city. While it could be argued that governments have an important role to play in protecting vulnerable residents in gentrifying areas from displacement, there are very few instances of this being done. In fact, not only do neoliberal governments often actively pursue entrepreneurial policies involving partnerships with the private sector as they seek capital investment in the city and its infrastructure, but they are also frequently at the forefront of metropolitan plans and strategies explicitly designed to move disadvantaged residents out of areas earmarked for redevelopment and gentrification. Such strategies may also involve the active policing of public space. The consequences, as Anne R. Roschelle and Talmadge Wright (2003: 149) suggest, can be devastating:

> Urban policies that lead to rapid gentrification of the city have displaced the poor and working people for years. However, recent increases in disparities of wealth combined with a reduction in the social wage, adequate health care, and the decline of affordable housing have forced the poor and homeless out of desirable public space, isolating them in peripheral neighbourhoods and in shelters.

Indeed, Wilson (2008) argues that when combined with the withdrawal of government welfare programmes since the 1980s and the institutionalization and localization of 'anti-poor' rhetoric and policies that have occurred from the 1990s, the result is a worsening of living conditions within city ghettoes and an increased marginalization of both the ghetto and its residents.

## Conclusion

There is an incontrovertible connection between the growth, structuring and physical form of the modern city and economic processes and flows, particularly those associated with industrial and financial capitalism. It was the industrial revolution in Europe in the eighteenth and nineteenth centuries that transformed towns and small cities of the global North into heaving metropolises. Conversely, it was deindustrialization in the 1980s and 1990s that again transformed many of these same cities because financial capital was withdrawn and (frequently iconic) industries were closed. Neoliberalism, the growth of the global economy and the associated dominance of the financial sector have in different ways been pivotal to building new cities and urban environments and reconfiguring established ones, with the growth of the megacities of the South and the global dominance of financial centres such as London and New York City being noteworthy. In each case, the contrast between the resulting landscapes of wealth and those of poverty is highly visible. The spectacular spaces (enclaves) of prosperity and affluence are often located alongside, or indeed have been built on, the spaces of poverty, deprivation and decline (ghettoes and slums). What is revealed is the materiality or built texture of the city and the engraining of the processes of capitalism. It was such issues, consequences and relationships that were considered in this chapter. These themes are now continued into the next chapter, which probes the spatiality or materiality of diversity, inequality and homogeneity.

# 3
# Everyday City
## Diversity and Predictability

> The simplest [definition] is that a city is a human settlement in which strangers are likely to meet. For this definition to hold true, the settlement has to have a large heterogeneous population; the population has to be packed together rather closely; market exchanges among the population must make this dense, diverse mass interact.
>
> Sennett 1978: 39

## Introduction

The city is where difference is both created and most likely to be tolerated. It is, as Richard Sennett succinctly puts it in the passage above, the meeting place of strangers, although it should be noted that the impetus for these 'meetings' may be as much social as economic. Density and heterogeneity no longer satisfactorily define 'the city', but they are, nevertheless, central to the experience of urbanism. As a result, one of the most critical challenges facing contemporary cities is effectively to support, and manage the consequences of, the diversity of their populations. At stake is the toleration of difference and the provision of spaces where people from a range of racial and cultural backgrounds can work, live, mingle and express their cultures and values. Also relevant is the equitable distribution of urban resources. Too often, however, the lived reality diverges from the ideal and, far from looking for ways and places to encounter difference, people actively try to avoid it. Different social classes increasingly inhabit different parts of the city for work, home and leisure; they trace different paths through urban space, and are keen that there be no unexpected encounters with the 'other'. For the contemporary city dweller, the ideal urban environment is often one that is controlled, homogeneous and predictable – a space of managed diversity that floats free of density. This city is not a place where difference is celebrated but one of watchfulness and suspicion comprised of enclaves of homogeneity where interacting with strangers is eschewed.

The relationship between cities, homogeneity and difference is the concern of this chapter, which, in its contemplation of urban diversity, frequently draws attention to the inner city and to public space as the sites where the complexity of urban life is most readily revealed. The chapter examines some of the ways in which public space is understood within urban studies before going on to consider creative city and creative class strategies for reshaping public space and the public sphere that have gained currency and which are representative of a number of high-profile city reimaging treatises focused on urban diversity, creativity and the public realm. In this context, the chapter also considers claims that rather than fostering diversity, such initiatives are predicated on the marginalization of the 'other' and are blueprints for gentrification and conspicuous consumption. Finally, the chapter examines suburbia, which is often positioned as the antithesis of the heterogeneous city – a supposedly bland and undifferentiated physical, demographic and discursive space. Such conceptualizations are unsustainable, however, as the suburbs have been revealed to be complex spaces fractured by contradictory discourses, population profiles and experiences.

## Public space and its uses

When urban sociologists first turned their attention to issues of heterogeneity or diversity in the city, their concern was to describe the zones within cities that are occupied by different social, racial and ethnic groups. This was a focus of the Chicago School. Others explained difference in terms of class, gender and urban stratification. In an era of mass migration and when a substantial proportion of the residents of any major city may well have been born elsewhere, the emphasis has shifted again and the concern is twofold. The first concern is to understand what increased racial and ethnic diversity means for social and cultural cohesion within cities; in other words, to address the challenges that come with 'living together' in the context of difference. Indeed, as Stuart Hall (1993: 361) suggests, 'the capacity to live with difference is . . . the coming question of the 21st century'. The second concern is to probe the role of diversity in the enlivenment of the city (and its suburbs) and in shaping a productive cosmopolitanism. A number of interesting concepts have developed in this context, with Leonie Sandercock's metaphor of the 'mongrel city' being perhaps the most evocative in pointing to the complexity of a 'new urban condition in which difference, otherness, fragmentation, splintering, multiplicity, heterogeneity, diversity, plurality prevail' (Sandercock 2003: 1). Sandercock talks optimistically of the possibility of developing urban policy and planning approaches that are grounded in a 'multicultural sensibility'. Others focus on the possibilities that are inherent in the 'intercultural city' (Wood and Landry 2008). The city, it is also claimed, is where the freedom to be different is possible, as Georg Simmel (1995) famously argued at the start of the twentieth century.

In this context, cosmopolitanism, 'understood as implying a particular stance towards difference in the world, one that involves an openness to, and tolerance of, diversity' (Young et al. 2006: 1687), emerges as one of the most interesting and recurring concepts used in recent attempts to theorize the contemporary city in terms of difference. In examinations of cities and urban life, cosmopolitanism, as a form of urban subjectivity, fuses with the concept of the cosmopolitan city. And public space – its uses, purpose, design and management – is often at the centre of discussions of, and engagement with, cosmopolitanism and diversity. Indeed, public space as the location of encounters with difference is often bracketed with cosmopolitanism as a 'foundational element of any city' (Sassen 2010a: 490). It is where 'differing diversities' (Bennett 2001) are at their most obvious and, potentially, most volatile.

Visitors to Jaume Plensa's Crown Fountain in Chicago's Millennium Park on a hot afternoon will have witnessed the delight of children playing in its water sprays and been transfixed by the random faces projected on the fountain's columns. The fountain is not only an arresting piece of video sculpture and public art, but it is also a central element in creating what, to the visitor at least, appears to be a dynamic and successful public space. Sharon Zukin (1997: 259) observes that '[p]ublic spaces are the primary sites of public culture; they are a window into a city's soul.' Even allowing for a degree of hyperbole, there can be no doubt that the quality, use and presence of urban public space is central to the way in which people experience and relate to the city as resident or visitor, and whether encountering it in the context of work, education or leisure (to name but three). Public spaces are also deeply linked to the development and maintenance of civic culture. Parks, footpaths, beaches, the verges

3.1   A street market in Florence, Italy.

of rivers and waterways are all important in this respect, as are roads and thoroughfares – the sites of intersection, movement and transportation. What is understood as public space also embraces publicly funded institutions, including museums, libraries and galleries (many of which have free entry), and town halls and civic centres, as well as leisure spaces, such as swimming pools. These are the places that are owned collectively by residents and managed by local councils, state or national governments, and are entwined with ideas of citizenship and urban culture. But it is important to broaden the conceptualization of public space beyond one of ownership and to understand it as shared urban space. Reframed thus, public space also includes department stores, 'main streets' and other urban places where large numbers of people congregate for a range of purposes, including recreation, debate, consumption and entertainment. Shared space, be it publicly or privately owned, is the location for everyday encounters with difference/strangers.

In a similar vein, Fran Tonkiss (2005: 67) usefully divides public space into three ideal-types – the square, the café and the street – which, she argues, characterize 'three different senses of being with others in public'. Here the 'square' refers to those spaces provided by the state and used collectively, which are routinely associated with the concept of public space and are central to producing a sense of place identity and of belonging to a particular town or city. The 'café', by contrast, refers to the places of everyday social engagement, including theatres, restaurants, bars, coffee shops and churches, which are not necessarily or indeed usually in public ownership. As Tonkiss (2005: 67) explains, it is 'not a question of who owns it, exactly, but of the sense of public life it engenders'. Finally, 'the street' is the site of a complex of everyday, incidental encounters – 'the basic unit of public life in the city' (Tonkiss 2005: 68) – popularized by the noted urban commentator Jane Jacobs (1993/1961) in her evocative account of 'the uses of sidewalks'.

Tonkiss also points to a view that links the shared spaces of social exchange with the idea of an engaged and democratic 'public sphere', and she notes the influence of the work of prominent sociologist Jürgen Habermas (1991/1962) in this respect. In line with his complex theory of communicative action, Habermas regards the public sphere as a site of debate and (rational-critical) discourse that mediates between the private sphere of everyday life and the state. According to his thesis, the public sphere is a set of social institutions and practices that emerged with the development of urban bourgeois society from the eighteenth century and comprises communication and information sources such as newspapers, as well as many of the forms of public space that Tonkiss discusses. Habermas (1996/1992: 374) proffers a tripartite conceptualization for his understanding of the public sphere, which he argues is

> differentiated into levels according to the density of communication, organizational complexity, and range – from the *episodic* publics found in taverns, coffee houses, or on the streets; through the *occasional* or 'arranged' publics of particular presentations and events, such as theatre performances, rock concerts, party assemblies, or church congresses; up to the *abstract* public sphere of isolated readers, listeners, and viewers scattered across large geographic areas, or even around the globe, and brought together only through the mass media.

The public sphere is not coterminous with public space, although it is often treated as such, but it does embrace elements of spatiality.

Influential British policy commentator Geoff Mulgan (1989) has observed that there is a link between politics and civic and public space that can be traced back to the Greek *polis*. He is concerned that the 'cultural roots of democratic, public life' are being threatened by the increased privatization of public space which is an outcome of neoliberalism (Mulgan 1989: 276). At issue here is not shared social space in its broadest sense, but those spaces that are publicly owned and freely used – gardens, squares and civic spaces. Mulgan (1989: 275) argues that '[a]ny plans for the creation of convivial, communicating cities inevitably find themselves struggling with a long erosion of the traditional political structure of the city within which people think, argue and organise.' Mulgan's position is representative of a view well established in urban cultural studies that holds that the public spaces of earlier times were places where ideas were exchanged and public engagement occurred. This position is well summarized in the following passage from the influential (and tellingly titled) book *City Centres, City Cultures*:

> What is at issue here is the gradual erosion of public space, or the 'civic realm' . . . that geographical and historical space in our towns and cities that properly belongs to the residents as a community in the form of town squares, public gardens, street markets and meeting places. . . . Increasingly, people come into the town as isolated and individual consumers; rarely as active citizens or members of a civic community. (Bianchini et al. 1988: 11)

The idea that civic culture is something forged in the inner city is apparent in many guises in the literature on public space, and it is suggested, for example, that the reclamation and revival of public space is critical to the reconstruction of local meanings and identity believed to be central to an empowering experience of urbanism (Worpole 1992: 4–6). Mulgan (1989: 264) asserts that,

> alongside new policies for housing, transport and education, the new vision of the city will also emphasise its nature as a means of communication, a place where people meet, talk and share experiences, where they think and drink together. Cities work only if they are places where people engage in a collective process of making meanings and defining their place in the world.

It is significant, given the way in which the suburbs are frequently regarded (see below), that this focus on city centres occurs to the exclusion of the other spaces of the city, public or otherwise. The crux of the argument appears to be that the revitalization of the inner city and the reconstruction and reclamation of its public spaces are pivotal to the revival of local democracy and for the fostering of a strong civic culture. The other aim is to engage those supposedly isolated individuals who either have come to the inner city as consumers or have shunned the inner city for the (supposedly homogeneous) dormitory and retail spaces of suburbia and for the leisure pursuits which are now available within the private home. There are several important assumptions implicit here. First, it seems to be presumed that collective and subjective meanings of place and identity are not being constituted and 'community' is not being made and experienced in the myriad of other places of the city, including the much-maligned suburbs and the shared social spaces of the inner and outer city. Second, it is implied that a personal or civic identity derived from, or consolidated by, the inner city is in some way superior to, or more authentic than, one derived from these other spaces. Third, there is tacit belief that all groups are able to use, and have equal access to, the public spaces of the city centre. This assumption is based on the highly questionable view that all groups used these spaces equally in the past.

In other words, the public spaces of the inner city are privileged over those of elsewhere, and the significant local or micro politics that pervades other urban sites is being overlooked. Absent is an acknowledgement of the extent to which the city centre and the activities identified as taking place in its confines have often been dominated by a minority of the population: white, middle-class, middle-aged men. There is also little acknowledgement of the places of women and their politics, which traditionally are located somewhere other than the city centre. In recent years, a number of high-profile city revival strategies have also become implicated in discussions of urban space and the public sphere in ways that fuse notions of local citizenship with the idea and reality of the city centre and its public spaces, with the work of Mulgan, Bianchini and others (discussed above) being influential. These ideals often also find expression in a raft of formal and informal competitions between cities to attract tourists and investment capital (Lovatt and O'Connor 1995; Stevenson 1998). Liveability, vitality, city image, as well as public space and the public sphere, all come to the fore as cities attempt to introduce strategies that will mark them as distinctive and attractive places for people to live, work and visit. The city centre is frequently the focus of strategies which variously aim to animate public space, build the civic sphere and foster diversity. At the same time, there has been a rise in the number of consultants offering city reimaging and civic revival 'toolkits' and blueprints (Stevenson 2004), with Richard Florida (2003, 2004) and Charles Landry

(2006) being two high-profile exponents. Most of these blue-prints pivot on a rather predictable suite of recommenda-tions, with most prioritizing three interconnected ingredients: place, citizenship and creativity (Stevenson forthcoming).

## Reimaging and the 'creative city'

With the decline of a city's industrial base frequently comes the decline of its public and private spaces and wealth-gen-erating capacity. It was the decline of traditional industrial cities in the United Kingdom in the 1980s that initially prompted an interest in the role that the cultural industries could play in urban revitalization. At the heart of city reim-aging approaches is the proposition that successful cities are those where public space is lively, and creativity in all things, including the operation of the market, thrives – 'creativity', argue Landry and Bianchini (1995: 11), and civic creativity in particular 'has always been the lifeblood of the city'. For Landry (2002: 167), 'Creative City strategy-making . . . [is] . . . holistic, valuing connections . . . people-centred rather than land use focused. This is because it is people's skills and creativity which drive urban develop-ment.' Creative city making is thus both a process and a way of thinking. It is, in Landry's (2002: 239) view, reflexive and evaluative. There are many indicators, concepts, techniques and matrices in this particular toolkit. Significant, though, is Landry's linking of the creativity of individuals with that of the urban and the civic, which he has spelt out more recently:

> [C]reativity . . . in the context of individuals [is about the] capacity to think across boundaries . . . to grasp the essence of an issue. . . . [T]o think through and implement a *creative city* agenda . . . involves conjoining the interests and power of different groups . . . [and the ability] to learn to work in partnership between different sectors that share mutual respect, and, most importantly, to develop civic creativity. (Landry 2006: 400)

So, overarching the creative city agenda is an emphasis on ethics and establishing the values on which being a creative city is based. The challenge seemingly is to move beyond narrow concerns with a single city and its promotion, to become what Landry (2006: 335) terms a 'creative city for the world' that is focused on environmental, social and cultural sustainability and which connects 'creativity to bigger picture aims'. John Montgomery (2008), a former colleague of Landry and another of the original advocates of placing creativity at the centre of city and civic building, also presents a model for the development of successful cities. This model pivots on the premise that such cities 'retain in balance a creative and dynamic economy, an innovative cultural life and a "good fit" of the built form to activity' (Montgomery 2008: 4). As he further points out, since the 1980s the urban planning and development agenda of a vast number of cities has been one that endeavours to combine economic development and innovation, cultural vitality and urban 'place-making'. For Montgomery, cities are economic entities which are built and thrive as trading hubs. Consistent with neoliberal approaches, his core premise is that those cities with strong economies are also culturally vibrant centres of creativity and innovation – great arts movements, he suggests, are almost always urban and emerge in the context of strong economic growth. '[B]ursts of wealth creation and city development occur in particular places at particular times because of the development of new technologies which give rise to new industries, new production processes and new art forms' (Montgomery 2008: 10). For Montgomery the world economy is now on the cusp of a new wave of economic growth which will be centred on culture, the knowledge economy and the emerging digital industries. He claims the challenge is clear: 'Cities that manage to combine some representation of some of these industries with high levels of artistic creativity and design will also flourish. These will be the successful cities of the fifth wave, plus any others that find a creative niche' (Montgomery 2008: 368).

Also relevant is Richard Florida's (2003) highly influential supply-side treatise on the so-called urban 'creative class' and its role in regenerating cities and regions. In effect, Florida's is a formula for urban renewal and economic prosperity that, according to one commentator, pivots on adopting urban policies that will 'attract, retain and even pamper a mobile and finicky class of "creatives", whose aggregate efforts have become the primary drivers of economic development' (Peck 2005: 740). This creative class is made up of a core group that includes people engaged in such fields as the arts, research and science, and a peripheral group that comprises those working in fields including law, health, business and finance (Florida 2003: 8). The creative class is defined by its ability to be innovative and flexible in its work. It is also (supposedly) highly, often globally, mobile. In Florida's schema, this class chooses to live and work in those places where diversity is accepted and which offer appropriate 'opportunities and amenities' (Florida 2003: 11). In order to be economically prosperous, argues Florida, cities must develop the urban, social, cultural and economic infrastructure that will attract this creative class. It is the presence of the creative class in a city that supposedly enlivens it and makes it a place where businesses will want to locate. In Florida's view, therefore, cities should invest in the infrastructure that will attract the creative class, rather than, as is usually the case, offer incentives, such as tax breaks, in the hope of attracting business. Florida turns established assumptions around by arguing that it is the creative class (and not business) that comes first and is the key to urban and economic (and social and cultural) prosperity. As the creative class is apparently attracted to the 'creative city', Florida encourages cities to develop regeneration strategies that prioritize the building of art galleries, restaurants, cultural precincts and other forms of 'soft' creative infrastructure, including public space, pedestrianization, street lighting and street furniture.

In many ways, this is a simple formula, which, as Jim McGuigan (2009) points out, mobilizes culture in the service of economic development. Jamie Peck (2005: 741) further suggests that Florida 'mixes cosmopolitan elitism and pop universalism, hedonism and responsibility, cultural radicalism and economic conservatism, casual and causal inference, and social libertarianism and business realism'. The creative class formula is also a recipe for gentrification and the displacement of lower-income (non-creative class) residents, often including, ironically, artists and creative workers (see Chapter 2). The spaces that the creative class is attracted to are those in, or near, the city centre, which, as discussed in

3.2    Redeveloped inner-city laneways, Melbourne, Australia.

Chapter 2, are often poorer working-class neighbourhoods or ghettoes. And while an aim of this blueprint is to foster diversity, the result can be the opposite – the serial reproduction of sameness.

Irrespective of gentrification and displacement, a successful creative city strategy is understood as being one that achieves a range of social, economic and urban, as well as creative, outcomes, including rejuvenating public space and the public sphere. Particularly enticing is the idea that a creative cities approach can address many of the seemingly intractable problems confronting former industrial cities. Indeed, the stimulation of a vibrant urban economy based on consumption (as opposed to production) is often represented as a sure-fire way to revitalize towns and cities (particularly declining city centres and 'high streets') and to make the inner city safe at night (see Chapter 4). This is a trend that has been particularly evident in provincial cities that were once dependent on manufacturing and heavy industry but which now seek entrepreneurial solutions to address the substantial social and economic problems caused by the withdrawal of capital.

The approaches of Florida, Landry, Montgomery and others, grounded as they are in intriguing combinations of urban planning, economics, sociology and motivational psychology, have proved to be seductive, accessible and highly marketable – local governments around the world being eager to '[do] a Florida thing' (McGuigan 2009). These consultants and their blueprints have successfully captured the attention of civic leaders, artists and urban planners alike and been influential in shaping not only local approaches to urban redevelopment and reimaging, but also debates about the idea of the city and what is meant by 'city-ness' and civic culture. Culture and creativity have thus become currencies – forms of capital – that supposedly can be measured, developed and then traded in an international marketplace comprised of cities eager to compete with each other on the basis of image, amenity, liveability and visitability (Richards and Palmer 2010). Such factors have also been influential in prompting the emergence of formal and informal, national and international competitions for creative city status, the most notable of which is the European Union's Capital of Culture competition.

The EU has initiated a number of city-focused contests as part of its aim to forge a pan-European sense of identity. To some extent the focus on cities and on linking, promoting and celebrating them circumvents member nation states and the politics of national governments by establishing direct links with as well as between cities. So, on the European agenda, cities matter, as does local culture (broadly defined). The EU Capital of Culture competition is a transnational approach that directly targets and supports the local. It was in this context, for instance, that EUROCITIES was established in 1986 as a network of 120 major European cities from more than thirty European countries. The EURO-CITIES network operates on the basis that because the decisions and initiatives of the European Union directly affect cities and their local communities, it is appropriate for the EU to put in place mechanisms and schemes to support urban life, cities and their priorities and experiences (Griffiths 1995). EUROCULT21 was one such initiative, being conceived in the early twenty-first century as an alliance of European city authorities, academic and research institutions from different countries and cross-European networks, including EUROCITIES. It was, however, the naming of Glasgow in 1990 as the European City of Culture (known from 1999 as the European Capital of Culture) that was really pivotal, first, in focusing international attention on this particular inter-urban competition and, second, in highlighting the potential usefulness of the scheme to deindustrialized cities that were keen to reposition their image and economies.

Indeed, the Glasgow example became the referent for other cities that were also not traditionally associated with culture and creativity. It became emblematic of the so-called 'benefits' that could flow to those cities that assertively placed the arts, cultural industries and tourism at the centre of their renewal and economic recovery strategies. Glasgow's City of Culture status was but one element in a range of interlinked local initiatives that had been put in place over a number of years, including upgrading the built environment, opening new cultural institutions (notably the Glasgow Concert Hall and the Tramway performance spaces) and staging a programme of flagship festivals. A number of government-sponsored community housing projects were also implemented, historic buildings were restored and new office spaces were constructed. It was a significant exercise in city reimaging/rebranding (see Chapter 7). However, assessing the nature and extent of Glasgow's so-called 'success' has not been straightforward. There is, for instance, no developed agreed methodology for evaluating more broadly the legacy of a range of culture-led urban regeneration approaches. Nevertheless, the evidence suggests that creative city strategies often fail to develop cultural infrastructure beyond the city centre. Some have raised concerns that such approaches may well result in a hardening of the geography of inequality and do little to foster local community development. Such criticisms have certainly been made of Glasgow (Miller 2012). Nevertheless, the Glasgow example continues to be a potent and much-cited and -copied example for culture-led approaches to urban redevelopment and reimaging, and the competition to be named as a European Capital of Culture continues to be fierce.

Diversity and creativity strategies and discussions within urban studies are very much focused on the city centre. They thus shape a perception that privileges these zones and marginalizes others – the seemingly non-urban areas of the city, in particular, the suburbs which are viewed as homogeneous and 'non-creative'. The creative class supposedly is not attracted to the suburbs. As cities and their populations change, however, there is a need to consider not only whether the suburbs have ever been the bland spaces they are routinely positioned as, but also what the consequences are or might be of the changing shape of the city for life in the suburbs.

## The suburbs and beyond

Suburbs – those residential or 'dormitory' zones located away from the city centre – have been part of the urban landscape probably from the earliest days of city building (Phelps et al. 2010). But it was during the nineteenth century that the suburbs emerged as prominent as middle-class residents of English industrial cities escaped the squalid and overcrowded conditions of inner-city areas of the type in Manchester so graphically described by Engels (see Chapter 2) for the cleaner and less congested neighbourhoods that ringed the city. An outcome of post-war prosperity and before the widespread gentrification of the inner city, residency in the suburbs was a marker of affluence and social class. It was also in response to the filthy urban conditions created by industrialism, along with the perceived debauchery of inner-city life, that Ebenezer Howard (1965/1902) developed his highly influential proposal for the Garden City, which, although not a prescription for suburbia *per se*, nevertheless, was a rejection of the city and a celebration of a decentralized low-density urban form that, over time, merged both discursively and in many urban planning proposals with the idea of the suburb.

Howard's vision for the ideal city was one of self-contained urban villages ringed by farms and gardens. Neither rural nor urban, this was a third type of settlement that supposedly combined the attractions of the city (jobs, high wages and social opportunity) with the sunshine, fresh air and 'natural' environments of the country. Howard's Garden Cities were to have total populations of approximately thirty thousand living in designated residential zones housing two thousand people (Howard 1965/1902). Also part of Howard's original vision for the Garden City was the collective ownership of property; but this was an apparently politically unpalatable idea that was soon abandoned (Short 1991: 87–88). Neither Howard, nor the Garden City movement his ideas fostered, 'invented' the suburbs or the now-pervasive planning notions of 'green-belts', 'garden suburbs' and 'urban villages', but there can be no doubt that this work was influential, if not in popularizing these ideals, then in providing the intellectual terrain on which they developed. The Garden City movement was also instrumental in prompting the development of formal urban planning processes, including the introduction of land-use zoning. Suburbanization to a very great extent assumed, and became code for, decentralization, low population densities and single-use zoning.

Following the Second World War the landscapes of cities in Western nations around the world were reshaped by levels of suburbanization that occurred on an unprecedented scale – indeed, urbanization became, in effect, *sub*urbanization. This rapid suburban growth was also accompanied by a 'baby boom', increased levels of household affluence resulting from 'full' (male) employment and rising wages as an outcome of the post-war economic boom, and the mobility and residential choice that came with high levels of private car ownership. As a result, suburban life became attainable not only by the middle class but also by many in the working class as well (Nicolaides 2002; Wiese 2004). And if it was not attainable, the dream was alluring. The suburbs came to be associated with nuclear families, economic prosperity, job security and the 'good life' – the stuff of popular television programmes and women's magazines (Stevenson 2003). A house in the suburbs was where workers and their families aspired to live. In Australia, which is arguably the most suburbanized nation in the world, the suburban form and its associated lifestyle also fused with the aspiration of home ownership to become an important marker of national and individual success. The suburbanization of home ownership built what Brendan Gleeson (2006) terms the 'Australian heartlands'.

**3.3  Suburbia, Sydney, Australia.**

Mass suburbanization not only reshaped the post-war urban landscapes of the West, but it shifted quite significantly the focus and tenor of the debate about cities and urban life, with most urban commentators being highly critical of the emerging suburbia, which they dismissed (vilified) for its car dependency, and demographic and social homogeneity. For instance, in 1961, Lewis Mumford (1989/1961: 509), although an advocate of decentralization, nevertheless described the suburbs as the 'anti-city' – places where 'speed and empty space' were worshipped, while in the same year, Jane Jacobs (1993/1961: 273), the doyenne of urbanism, opined that the suburbs may well be 'viable and safe' but they were 'apt to be dull' because they do 'not generate city liveliness or public life'. According to the many critics of suburbia, the suburbs fail to offer a rich quality of life, a choice of entertainment facilities and social diversity because of their residential profile and lack of density. Others claim that suburban life is not only monotonous but also 'individualistic and selfish' (Wilson 2001: 105). The suburbs have also been criticized because of the environmental destruction they supposedly cause (Glaeser 2011; Hayden 2004), the quality and characteristics of their housing stock, and the physical layout of their estates. In arguing that the suburbs (or at least those of Australia in the 1950s and 1960s) were aesthetic and intellectual wastelands, the architect Robin Boyd (1968) expressed sentiments that were fairly typical of the views of those who were committed to the aesthetic and design principles of modernism. The negative appraisal of suburbia has also been played out over many years in the creative arts, literature and the popular media in a host of shifting, sometimes contradictory, ways (Craven 1995; Devine-Glass 1994). 'Suburban' became code for the boring, the banal and the self-indulgent.

Observing the increased suburbanization of the black middle class in the United States, William Julius Wilson (1987) has argued that it is a trend that exacerbated the marginalization and disadvantage of the black urban poor left behind in declining inner-city neighbourhoods. Mary Pattillo-McCoy (2000) builds on Wilson's work to highlight the complexity not only of the African American middle class (as a socio-economic category and set of 'normative judgements'), but also of its residential choices and location, suggesting that the suburbanization of the black middle class is a product of the increased size of the class rather than a rise in its movement (migration) out of the inner city. This suburbanization does not, however, mean racial integration and the proliferation of mixed-race neighbourhoods; rather, it has overwhelmingly meant either the development of predominantly black middle-class neighbourhoods or the movement of the white middle class to other neighbourhoods when the black middle class move in.

Looking at the history of suburbanization and race from a different perspective, Andrew Wiese (2004) has demonstrated that there is a long tradition of working-class black Americans also seeking to live in the suburbs, attracted by the same combination of ideological, structural and social factors that made these areas appealing to middle-class white Americans. He goes on to argue that for many working-class black Americans, suburban home ownership is seen as a way of 'adapting to urban capitalism' – 'a basis for economic survival' (Wiese 2004: 69). And where, historically, the middle class could afford a house in the suburbs on the income of a sole (male) breadwinner, the working class almost always relies on two incomes. As home ownership and home equity are often the primary, even sole, asset of many black working-class families, it is easy to see why they, along with poor Latino home owners, were hit hardest by the recent housing/mortgage crisis in the United States. Jacob S. Rugh and Douglas S. Massey (2010) also see levels of race-based residential segregation as key factors leading to the foreclosure crisis in American cities.

In the 1970s a strong feminist critique of suburbia emerged which claimed that it was deeply implicated in the subordination of women. According to this view, women were disadvantaged by suburban life and, in particular, by the separation of work and home that was entrenched in suburbia (Wilson 2001). Many feminists also pointed to the high levels of violence against women that were part of the domestic landscape of the suburbs. The starting point for feminist critiques of suburbia was the observation that even though men and women lived in the same houses, neighbourhoods and suburbs, they occupied different spaces for work and leisure. Central here is what is called the 'gender division of labour', whereby men and women traditionally perform very different roles in society, with men travelling to work each day and women remaining at home to take charge of the household and care for children and elderly relatives. The spatial implication of the gender division of labour was that the suburbs came to be regarded as the 'natural' spaces for women and children, while the city was the place of working men. In other words, the modern industrial city was regarded as being divided into discrete male and female zones (McDowell 1983; Matrix 1984; Saegert 1980). Breaking the shackles of suburbia was seen by second-wave feminists as essential to the liberation of women.

In an influential book entitled *The Levittowners*, the American urban sociologist Herbert Gans (1967) utilized the method of participant observation to examine life in a post-war American suburb. Contrary to the dominant view at the time, Gans found that this suburb was not a place of bland conformity and homogeneity at all; rather, he argued, it was 'beset' with class and generational divisions and conflicts.

The suburbs, according to Gans, were characterized by pluralism and tension, albeit occurring at very different scales from what was experienced in the inner city. Gans also highlighted the important role of everyday struggle and agency in shaping the social worlds of suburban dwellers, and in this he argued strongly against spatial determinist perspectives that suggested that particular environments caused certain (hence predictable) types of behaviour and social outcomes. Interestingly, Gans went on to claim that because of a range of entrenched social and political factors, including dominant stereotypes of suburban harmony and homogeneity, suburbanites were actually ill equipped and thus unable to deal with the (unexpected) diversity they encountered in their neighbourhoods.

In the 1960s, Gans was something of a lone voice in identifying and describing the lived dimensions of suburban complexity. But these sentiments coalesced to some extent with a suspicion which was starting to gain currency in some quarters that beneath its supposedly bland exterior, the suburbs harboured the same seething underbelly that many had come to suspect was also lurking in country towns (Stevenson 2003). Elizabeth Wilson (2001: 111) argues in this context that the 'discovery' that the suburbs had a 'dark side' in fact contributed to the ambivalence with which they are viewed:

> There is a fascination in the discovery that about 90 per cent of punk bands came from the suburbs. The suburbs are no longer seen as anonymous, boring and conformist. In the new myth, suburban couples take part in wife-swapping parties. Bored suburban housewives become part-time sex workers. The suburb is the haunt of the paedophile, even the mass murderer. Terrorists hide out there.

There has also been another shift recently in city–suburbia discourses, particularly in the cultural industries, where many creative producers who grew up in the suburbs are increasingly viewing them with nostalgia. So, while for many artists and commentators the suburbs, as the 'non-urban', remain an intellectual and cultural wasteland, for others they are the idealized spaces of childhood and potent sources of inspiration. The suburbs are also the places of creative production, as recent research has highlighted, and where large numbers of creative workers actually live (Collis et al. 2010). All the while, however, in the popular imagination this residential form continues to connect with powerful ideologies of the family, security, love, space and home as an idealized and highly sought-after residential environment.

In the period since the 1960s, such factors as increased migration (both international and domestic), shifting patterns of affluence, inner-city gentrification and significant population growth (although not necessarily the result of rising birth rates) have been influential in reshaping suburbia, to the extent that the suburbs of major Western cities are now much more socially and ethnically diverse than was previously the case. In addition, the social and economic status of women has also changed considerably since the 1960s, with increasing numbers of women entering the workforce; as a result, the suburbs, which were once the lively day-time spaces of non-working (married) women and their children, are now often quite deserted at this time (Richards 1990). Another important change has been the uncoupling of suburbia from low population densities and single-use zoning. In a trend that can perhaps be described as the 'urbanization of suburbia', many suburban zones now have high population densities, and an increasing number function as centres of commerce and employment in their own right, often having only a tangential relationship with the 'central' zones of the city. The suburbanization that has occurred in the cities of the South, in particular in China, India and Brazil, however, has been of a completely different order. Not only is it at densities not previously imagined let alone associated with suburbia, but also these cities sprawl across large regions forming networks of conurbations with multiple centres and no necessarily identifiable suburban periphery. Many ask whether these landscapes are suburbs at all. And the definitional confusion continues when one tries to categorize the 'arrival cities' and slums that have formed frequently on the edges of conurbations but also not uncommonly in zones much closer to the urban core.

Suburban densities in many cities of the North have also risen dramatically as these cities have grown to engulf vast geographical regions. Los Angeles is often regarded as emblematic of this trend, although New York City remains the most densely populated city in the United States (Burdett and Rode 2010: 18). Not unlike those of the South, the megacities of the North spread ever outward, claiming satellite cities, towns and farmland as they grow. It remains a matter of some conjecture, however, as to whether these claimed spaces become symbolically, economically and socially (as well as spatially) part of an ever-expanding suburbia organized (Chicago School style) around an identifiable centre – part of an entity that is 'a city' – or whether the idea of a dominant city and its subordinate suburbs has been rendered unsustainable. With reference to the Orange County district of Los Angeles, Rob Kling et al. (1995) label as 'postsuburban' those 'peripheries' that, they argue, have 'broken away' from the urban 'core' to become diverse and vibrant economic and cultural concentrations – cities – in their own right. The postsuburban comprises multi-centred regions 'organized around many distinct, specialized centers rather than a traditional city center surrounded by industrial and residential areas' (Kling et al. 1995: 6). Terms such as the 'global city-region' (Scott et al. 2001), 'edge cities' (Garreau 1991) and the 'endless city' (Burdett and Sudjic 2010), although not synonyms, are relevant in this context. At the level of policy, it is interesting to note by way of example that Sydney, Australia, usually considered one of the most highly suburbanized cities in the world, is regarded for planning purposes not as a 'City of Suburbs' but as a 'City of Cities' (New South Wales Department of Infrastructure, Planning and Natural Resources 2004), in recognition of its geographical size and multi-centred diversity. In contrast, however, Sydney City Council labels as the 'City of Villages' its particular local government area that resides within the multi-local government metropolis that is Sydney. Cities and villages, the rural and the urban: in the spaces of the margins, the suburban is rendered invisible.

For some, as Nicholas Phelps et al. (2010) point out, the new (sub)urban formation marks a clear break with the suburbia of the past while the traditional city comprising a core and a radiating periphery has been replaced by the multi-centred and the dispersed. This is a compelling proposition; however, it does not allow for the complexity and variety of the contemporary urban form. The suburbs of the metropolis can be dense, vibrant, diverse and autonomous; but they can also be low-rise, dormitory, monocultural and dependent. Cities can and do stretch across the landscape as vast multi-nodal conurbations; but they are also small and single-centred. In other words, it is not that one urban/suburban form has supplanted a prior form, but that new urban formations have developed alongside those that are more established – they are coterminous and often co-located. What is undeniable, though, is that the explanatory power of many established conceptual frames has ruptured as a result of the demographic and spatial realities of the contemporary city and suburbs. In particular, the core–periphery (binary) model of the city and the suburbs has been rendered partial, and heterogeneity rather than homogeneity needs to be more firmly placed at the centre of examinations of suburbia.

## Conclusion

The themes of this chapter were those of homogeneity and heterogeneity. It focused first on the centrality of public space (and its animation) to conceptualizations of urban diversity. Public space, public culture and the public realm have fused in many urban studies frameworks, whereby the public spaces of the inner city are celebrated as both marker and site of diversity, cosmopolitanism, creativity and democracy. In particular, these discourses and concerns have been mobilized through a raft of high-profile city visioning treatises. Most notable are those focused on the creative city and the creative class, and the edges of these strategies were traced in the chapter. It was argued, too, that many approaches rely implicitly on a dichotomy that posits the suburbs as the city's 'other'. The chapter then moved to discuss conceptualizations of the suburbs, suggesting that researchers have rarely grasped either the spatial and residential complexity of suburbia or the extent to which people value this residential form. The city–suburbia dichotomy is a complex one that is also underpinned by the rhythms of time – with the city centre traditionally being seen as the place of work and the day, and the suburbs the site of the night and the 'after-hours'. Night-time in the city is imagined as a time of excitement and danger, not of home and security. Just as the suburb as a lived and imaginative space is being rethought, so too is the city at night, and here the themes of homogeneity and heterogeneity again come to the fore. It is to an examination of these conceptualizations of the city that attention now turns.

# 4

# Dark City

## Regulation and Stimulation

> Cities . . . do not exhibit *one* problem in organized complexity, which if understood explains all. They can be analysed into many such problems or segments which, as in the case of the life sciences, are also related with one another.
>
> Jacobs 1993/1961: 564–5

## Introduction

Sunrise and sunset are times and spaces of considerable poignancy in any city. They are moments of transition which create, and are constituted through, a distinctive suite of spatio-cultural rhythms. Night to day; day to night. The 'start' and the 'end' of the day (and night) speak to the themes of expectation and change, as well as of predictability and routine. The rhythms of urban temporality shape those of urban space and urban life in a range of ways and highlight the simultaneity of segmentation and interconnection that Jane Jacobs refers to in the passage quoted above as being central features of the urban. During the so-called 'working week', which, in spite of changes to work, leisure and consumption, is still '9-to-5/Monday-to-Friday' in most cities around the world, the beginning and the end of the day are defined significantly by the rhythms of departure and arrival as day-time city workers travel between their places of work in the city and their homes in the suburbs. Transport systems frequently become choked, and the change of time configures specific movements through urban space. The nocturnal city is formed at the interface of the rhythms of temporality and seasonality as well as the discourses of stimulation and regulation.

This chapter examines the way in which the city after dark is regarded within urban studies. It begins by looking at the view that advocates stimulating urban night-time economy activity as part of a strategy to encourage people back to the inner city. This perspective often overlaps with treatises for the creative city and has been especially popular with de-industrializing cities, particularly in the United Kingdom and Australia, seeking to revive run-down inner cities and local economies. A consequence of this approach, however, has frequently been the creation of a night-time economy that is overly focused on entertainment precincts and alcohol consumption, creating the context for calls for increased surveillance and policing. In this view, the city at night has become a place of disorder and danger which needs to be controlled. Managing the struggle over the city at night and the contradictory objectives of stimulating and policing urban space and urban life are now amongst the most difficult and urgent tasks facing officials in cities around the globe. At the core of this challenge are questions of inclusion and exclusion, social justice, power and inequality. In this context, the chapter concludes with a consideration of gender and the quite contradictory relationships that women have with, and within, the city after dark.

## Spaces of the night-time economy

As the day-time city becomes the city of the night, the familiar spaces of work and leisure take on very different forms and functions. Many urban spaces that seem to be mundane, safe and occupied by day become abandoned and forbidding as the light moves through twilight into darkness, from the seemingly 'natural' to the 'artificial' (Schivelbusch 1988/1983). For instance, street furniture that has been installed for day-time use is often inappropriate or even dangerous at night. But where work dominates the discourses of the day-time city, it is the practices associated with leisure that have come to dominate the way in which the night city is lived and imagined. Work which takes place 'overnight' to ensure the city is ready for the next day, such as office cleaning, street sweeping and the like, is rendered invisible in most narratives of the city at night. What captures the popular imagination is leisure, and, in particular, the leisure that is associated with entertainment and excess. This is the leisure that occurs principally in hotels, bars and nightclubs, but also in restaurants, cinemas and theatres. It is sometimes illicit, and almost always disproportionately focused on alcohol consumption and the activities of young people.

In the context of his wide-ranging exposition of the production of space, Henri Lefebvre (1991/1974) suggests that abstract space is 'at once homogeneous and broken up', splintered by boundaries or 'fracture lines' that are, simultaneously or variously, political, symbolic and temporal. Abstract space, he argues, bears a range of socially constructed meanings, many of which relate to prohibition – subtle signs and symbols which operate frequently to 'protect the spaces of the rich' (Lefebvre 1991/1974: 319). But under conditions of prohibition and the spatial order created by capitalism will be found spaces and forms of sanctioned transgression. These are activities and uses of urban space that are officially and unofficially authorized to occur in selected places at certain times of the day – or night:

> Space is divided up into designated (signified, specialized) areas and into areas that are prohibited (to one group or another). It is further subdivided into spaces for work and spaces for leisure, and into daytime and night-time spaces. The body, sex and pleasure are often accorded no existence, either mental or social, until after dark, when the prohibitions that obtain during the day, during 'normal' activity, are lifted. This secondary and derivative existence is bestowed on them, at night, in sections of the city. . . . In accordance with this division of urban space, a stark contrast occurs at dusk as the lights come on in the areas given over to 'festivity', while the 'business' districts are left empty and dead. Then in a brightly illuminated night the day's prohibi-

tions give way to profitable pseudo-transgressions. (Lefebvre 1991/1974: 320)

*euphemizing act thru naming the area*

Night-time urban spaces are also often demarcated through the act of affixing labels, such as 'entertainment zone', 'eat street' and 'red-light district'. In designated after-dark zones, behaviour that may be regarded as antisocial in other spatio-temporal contexts is often not only permitted but promoted in an attempt either to contain such activities spatially or as part of a broader economic development strategy. Interesting in this context is Joanne Hanley's (2007) study of the way in which a local council used a strategy of spatial containment in an effort to control street prostitution in the face of opposition from middle-class residents who were keen to see their suburb gentrify and so wanted to change the way in which its streets were used at night. As Lefebvre (1991/1974: 321) argues, the breaking up or 'fragmentation' of space is very much about the exercise of power and the maintenance of control, but, of course, and as discussed below, night also provides opportunities for transgressions that may not be officially sanctioned.

In recent years, there has been a great deal of interest on the part of local authorities and 'concerned residents' in finding ways to foster 'vibrant' inner-city zones where visitors and locals feel welcome and safe at night. At the same time, there has also been a growing belief that this aim can be achieved through the development of a range of night-time activities and facilities that, in turn, will lead to positive economic outcomes for the city. Prompting this interest in the city at night were several interconnected factors, including, most notably, the physical and economic decline of many inner cities that is evidenced quite strikingly by increasing numbers of vacant shops and buildings and the appearance of general desolation (Stevenson 1998). This decline of the inner city was largely the result of significant changes in the patterns of retailing associated with the development of the suburban mega shopping mall, and the urban effects of deindustrialization. Also important, though, were the consequences for seemingly successful inner cities of focusing overly on day-time retailing and commercial activities, which meant that although these cities were thriving spaces by day, they became abandoned and often dangerous at night.

Many of the most influential proposals to revitalize the city after dark concentrate on stimulating night-time economic and social activities. Key concerns include developing entertainment precincts and fostering leisure industries (Stevenson 2004). According to this view, the most successful cities are those that provide a range of retail, residential and commercial facilities at the same time as nurturing population diversity, local cultures and the expressive arts. Some even go so far as to argue that city centres should be where sanctioned work and leisure activities take place twenty-four hours a day, seven days a week, twelve months a year. Indeed, in recent years the idea of the 'twenty-four-hour city' has gained considerable currency within the city reimaging literature and is at the heart of much thinking associated with inner-city precinct redevelopment and the drafting of strategies to ameliorate the problems of the city (Heath and Strickland 1997).

In some ways the idea of the twenty-four-hour city destabilizes the way cities and their rhythms have traditionally been thought about (Heath and Strickland 1997). Its underpinning rationale is to move away from a dominant dichotomous view that separates the activities that occur in a particular precinct in the day-time from those that occur at night. Once this dichotomy is established, all the strategic planning that is done seems to occur in relation to what are quite discrete fault-lines. There are, in effect, two separate cities imagined rather than one city with overlapping and intersecting functions. The city of the day and that of the night exist in parallel. The idea of the twenty-four-hour city is an attempt to break down these zonal and binary ways of thinking by starting from the premise that the city should be a place where a diversity of activities and facilities is on offer at the same and different times. It proceeds from the idea that 'things' should happen in the city at night and there are considerable economic benefits to be gained if they do. Twenty-four-hour inner-city precincts are framed quite explicitly as being spaces of consumption and cosmopolitanism, and it was in this context that the idea of the 'night-time' or 'evening' economy surfaced as important.

4.1   Temple Bar entertainment zone, Dublin, Ireland.

Franco Bianchini (1995), in an article based on his talk to the first Twenty-Four-Hour City Conference held in the United Kingdom in 1993, suggests that the idea of the night-time economy emerged in Europe in the late 1970s, when many cities, quite independently, moved explicitly to foster 'urban night-life'. For instance, according to Bianchini (1995: 122), in Rome in 1979 the staging of a successful programme of evening events prompted local politicians to argue in favour of the 'round-the-clock use of city centres'. Culture and entertainment, including the provision of more after-dark leisure facilities, quickly came to be regarded as capable of strengthening local economies and energizing those inner cities which either became abandoned at night after the shops and offices had closed for the day, or were in economic and physical decline.

Coalescing with this growing awareness of the potential of culture, entertainment and events to animate the city at night and support local economies were several other social factors which, in the late 1970s, led local authorities to try to address the so-called 'problems' of the night-time inner city. First, there was a general increase in local demand for more after-hours leisure and consumption facilities and activities, which was the direct result of rising disposable incomes, increased leisure time and the opening up of European universities to much greater numbers of students following the student protests of 1968. Indeed, university students became and continue to be 'an important new audience for night-time activities' (Bianchini 1995: 122). Second, and also following the events of 1968, there was an upsurge of new urban social movements which had strong cultural as well as political agendas and which, in turn, prompted increased interest in trying to achieve a range of broad social goals. In this context, Bianchini singles out the 'Reclaim the Night' marches and the associated demands of the women's movement as being particularly important.

Commencing in Philadelphia in 1975 and followed in 1977 by the first European march (held in Brussels), the now global Reclaim/Take Back the Night initiative was intended to highlight the problem of rape and sexual violence against women, including the specific dangers that women face in the city at night. (The position of women in the urban night-time is discussed further below.) It was in response to the demands of such social movements that many local politicians looked to 'animate' and populate the night-time city as a way of making its spaces safer. According to advocates of the stimulation approach to the night-time economy, the fundamental requirement for a successful inner city is the presence of people, and there is strong evidence that people feel safer and indeed are safer when there are others present either on the streets or living close by. The task as they saw it, therefore, was to attract different types of people to the city at all hours of the day and night – families, workers, tourists, people of varying ages, and those from a range of ethnic and racial backgrounds (Bianchini 1995; Lovatt and O'Connor 1995). Not all these people would necessarily use the place at the same time or in the same way, of course. But the idea was that at any one time there would be a mix and there would be activity.

Diversity is a central theme in the discourses of stimulating the night-time economy and creating the twenty-four-hour city. The key, it is argued, is to offer a range of facilities that will foster and cater to diversity. Examples include theatres, businesses, restaurants, nightclubs, artists' studios, student accommodation, middle-class apartments and hotels. Late-opening shops and night-time programmes at art museums are also often included in this mix, and having a range of different transportation modes is regarded as pivotal because transport enables people to get home easily after a night out.

One of the most influential early works on this subject was Ken Worpole's *Towns for People* (1992), which reported on a significant UK study of the changing nature of town centres. Worpole argued that in order to address the trans-formations that had occurred in work and leisure since the 1970s, it was necessary to alter the way that time and public culture and their relationship are viewed. He introduced the notion of 'time-shifting' to describe the process of moving/altering the times when urban activities occur to ensure that they fit better with people's needs and interests and help to generate a critical mass of activity in the city at different times. The rationale here was that rethinking the time when things happen in the city is a way of ensuring that places do not become desolate and dangerous, and of responding to significant transformations in the nature of society, including in the patterns of work and the increasing number of women in the workforce. To illustrate, Worpole provides several examples drawn from his study, including the sports and leisure centre that opens from 6.00 am to 2.00 am and the public library that extended its opening hours well into the evening in order to attract a wider cross-section of the local community. In a similar vein, it is becoming commonplace for major cultural institutions to offer night-time pro-grammes. For example, the Wednesday night Art After Hours initiative of the Art Gallery of New South Wales features a range of events such as film screenings, art lectures, ensemble performances and guided tours. There is also a music pro-gramme in the gallery's 'ArtBar' and all exhibitions and permanent collection displays are open on this night. In addi-tion, the Gallery offers a complimentary night bus service to nearby car parks and the city centre. More recently, the Australian Museum launched its Jurassic Lounge as a night-time programme of art, live music, drinks and other activi-ties, which it promotes as 'the Australian Museum as you've never seen it!' (http://www.jurassiclounge.com/, accessed April 2012).

The 'stimulation' view of the city after dark has obvious appeal to planners, local councils and business interests. It also, as Dick Hobbs et al. (2000) argue, fits with the shift in urban governance from service provision to entrepreneurialism that is associated with neoliberalism (see Chapters 2 and 7). What has quickly become evident, however, is that in many cities the ideal of the city at night often diverges from the lived reality. The most obvious outcomes of local strategies to foster the night-time economy (which in spite of the efforts of some cultural institutions is often focused on entertainment and has been accompanied by a relaxation of liquor licensing laws, including extending trading hours) have been a proliferation of licensed venues, an increase in alcohol consumption, the development of monocultural night-time leisure spaces and higher incidents of public disorder (Bavinton 2010). These outcomes contrast sharply with the notions of cosmopolitanism and the twenty-four-hour city that are at the core of 'stimulation' treatises. As a result, issues of law and order, policing and crime prevention have come to the fore in discussions about the city at night, which are often accompanied by the increasingly urgent demands of local residents to combat 'antisocial behaviour' and public violence (Chatterton and Hollands 2002). This second position dovetails with a wholly sceptical view of the night-time economy which argues that the city at night fosters a range of undesirable and criminal activities, such as public disorder, vandalism, physical assaults and alcohol-related injuries, illicit drug dealing and use, and sex work. It is such issues that concern local residents and divide the media, government officials and police, whose place in maintaining public order has partly been usurped by the expansion of new surveillance technologies and increased levels of private policing associated in particular with a range of 'bouncing' and security roles across the urban economy.

## Surveillance and policing

Cities, and particularly cities at night, have long been linked, both empirically and imaginatively, to criminality and devi-

*cities at night linked to crime & deviance* 

ance. This connection has assumed a somewhat potent complexion in recent years with the increased and often disorderly leisure-related use, and associated policing, of cityspace at night. At issue are licensed premises and designated entertainment precincts, many of which were developed as part of strategies to stimulate urban economies. This struggle over space is to some extent an outcome of the multifarious and dynamic relationship that exists between the social, cultural and material economies of cities and which, as discussed above, has, since the 1980s, emphasized consumption and lifestyle (Lovatt and O'Connor 1995). It is now widely accepted that many of the problems associated with night-time entertainment precincts are the outcome of monoculturalism and mono-activity, which in combination can be summarized quite simply as too many young people doing too much of one thing – drinking to excess (Chatterton and Hollands 2002). Hobbs et al. (2002), who separately and in combination have written extensively on this subject, discuss the situation of the former industrial city of Manchester in the north of England, a city which in the late 1980s/early 1990s aggressively fostered a culture and leisure approach to urban economic development. A central objective of this strategy was to stimulate the night-time economy through the expansion of inner-city leisure and entertainment infrastructure, including allocating late-night liquor licences.

By the beginning of the twenty-first century, an astonishing 75,000 people were going into inner Manchester every Friday and Saturday night for the purpose of leisure, much of it being related to the consumption of alcohol (Hobbs et al. 2002). Writing several years after Hobbs et al., John Montgomery (2008: 213) puts this figure at between 100,000 and 150,000 people and also points out that the number of licensed premises in central Manchester had doubled since 1992. The situation in many other former industrial northern British cities, such as Leeds and Nottingham, is comparable, and the majority now have inner-city night-time economy strategies that overwhelmingly privilege the sale of alcohol, often in large drinking barns that have late-night licences – the high-profile Walkabout hotel chain is one of the best known of these venues. In every case, by accident or design, it is young people who are disproportionately represented as patrons of the inner-city night-time economy.

In Australia, too, there has been considerable disquiet and debate in recent years about the desirability and consequences of designated night-time precincts which have become overly focused on alcohol consumption. In this context, perhaps one of the most interesting examples of the struggle over the use of night-time urban space is an initiative implemented in the deindustrialized regional city of Newcastle. Following the globally circulating blueprint, Newcastle actively sought to develop its night-time as part of a broader suite of initiatives implemented to rejuvenate its flagging economy and deal with an inner city that was routinely deserted after dark. Thus there was an increase in nightclubs and bars, many of which were granted extended trading licences, and, as also occurred in the United Kingdom, there was an associated marked increase in public drunkenness and disorder in the spaces of the after-hours city.

In an effort to deal with what then came to be seen as a law and order issue, and in response to considerable public disquiet, grounded in already-existing feelings of fear and risk commonly associated with the city at night and particular expressions of youthfulness and masculinity, the local council led a submission to the NSW Liquor Administration Board arguing for the introduction of a lockout and curfew in the inner city. This submission was successful and the curfew/lockout came into effect in March 2008. Under its terms, patrons are permitted to remain in a licensed establishment until it closes (at 3.00 am), but no one can enter a bar or nightclub once the 'lockout/lock in' starts at 1.00 am (Bavinton 2011). The aims of the initiative were, in part, to contain the consumption of alcohol within the spaces of licensed premises and to limit the movement of intoxicated people through public space in the early hours of the morning, including going between clubs and hotels. It is several years since the introduction of the Newcastle curfew and it is widely regarded as a success primarily because, according to police and crime statistics, there has been a considerable decrease in arrests – assault rates, for instance, reportedly dropped by 37 per cent in the two and a half years from March 2008. Although not the first Australian city to impose

4.2   Nightclub lockout sign, Melbourne, Australia.

such a curfew (Brabazon and Mallinder 2007), the perceived success of the Newcastle initiative has led to calls for other cities to introduce similar restrictions (http://www.abc.net. au/news/stories/2010/09/16/3013142.htm?site=newcastle, accessed April 2012).

Needless to say, however, the curfew approach has many opponents, with powerful hotel lobby groups being amongst the most vocal. There are others, though, who question the effectiveness and desirability of curfews and lockouts and argue that the problems of the inner city at night point to a lack of diversity and a failure of planning. In the United Kingdom, for instance, Montgomery (2008), who has been a high-profile advocate of the stimulation approach to urban revitalization, including most notably working on the revitalization of the 88-hectare Temple Bar precinct in inner Dublin (Montgomery 1995), discusses the problems that arise when the urban 'evening economy' becomes dominated by one social group and proposes what he regards as a solution. In Montgomery's view, the problem is not so much the night-time economy concept or indeed the twenty-four-hour city *per se* (although he does suggest that perhaps eighteen rather than twenty-four hours is long enough); rather, he argues that the dominance of the city at night by young people and alcohol is really the result of local authorities and regulators failing to 'determine how much late-night activity should be allowed, and where it should be located' (Montgomery 2008: 190). Montgomery goes on to assert that the answer lies in the better coordination of a range of policy and regulatory spheres, including town planning, transport and liquor licensing. Instead of taking a 'blanket' approach to precinct development and management, he proposes a precinct-specific (niche) strategy which nurtures a number of distinctive 'sub-areas' and a targeted range of activities and attractions (Montgomery 2008: 219).

Here Montgomery uses the example of Sunderland (another deindustrialized northern UK city), which has a night-time strategy centred on the development of four distinct inner-city zones each catering to specific groups of patrons. The aim is to encourage parallel diversity through a policy of fine-grained containment. Demographic data or crime statistics are not provided but it is highly likely that Sunderland's designated 'night-life quarter' is characterized by the same attractions and behaviour that have come to be associated more generally with the night-time economy. What is different is that other groups, such as families and theatregoers, are not encouraged to go to this zone for their night-time entertainment because this is being provided in one of the other quarters. There are also 'very few' people living in the night-life quarter (Montgomery 2008: 221). The Sunderland approach sanctions activities to occur within clearly demarcated precincts, which, of course, means the space and the activities that take place within it are more easily policed. Not unlike the curfew/lockout method and the street prostitution 'containment' strategy mentioned above, spatial containment intended to control behaviour and facilitate policing is the key to this approach.

The growth of urban economic development strategies explicitly designed to stimulate night-time leisure, and the associated emergence of new forms of policing, surveillance and regulation to control the resulting behaviour, have highlighted the central role of private security in the night-time economy and the tensions that exist between the public and the private, including in the management of public and private night-time space (Hobbs et al. 2002). Indeed, the private security staff – 'bouncers' – who patrol the entrances of entertainment venues play a particularly ambiguous and highly potent role in policing the city at night (Hobbs et al. 2002; Tomsen 1997). Hobbs et al. (2002: 355) detail the way in which the private has usurped the public in the policing of night-time space:

> As the day gives way to the night, the state relinquishes and devolves many of its policing duties to the bouncer. In the absence of public police officers, bouncers take responsibility for incorporating night-time visitors into the disciplines and protocols of the late-night leisure market. . . . [B]ouncers are permitted wide discretion in their task of imposing commercially, rather than legally or morally justifiable behavioural codes.

*the bouncer*

While most overt at night, the increasing use of private policing and surveillance encroaches into the day-time, being part of a significant shift in the struggle over urban space and the relationship between criminality and the city. It is in this context that the complex city/crime nexus becomes important, including the strategies being adopted to control those urban activities that are perceived by the mainstream as 'deviant'. Roy Coleman, for instance, discusses the pervasive use of surveillance strategies, in particular closed-circuit television (CCTV), to maintain control and public order in UK cities, highlighting that the British are now the most 'watched, catalogued and categorised people in the advanced world', something which, he suggests, has occurred with 'little public debate or opposition' (Coleman 2004: 3). In Coleman's view, CCTV has significantly altered the relationship between people and the city, and he asserts that some groups are targeted routinely for surveillance in order to make others (and their property) safe. He goes on to argue that the use of CCTV is rarely questioned either in the media or by public officials. Rather, its use is positioned unequivocally as being a good thing and in the public interest.

*T.V. surveillance*

Coleman argues that the justification for installing CCTV in the United Kingdom has been to 'reclaim' cityspace not only for the consuming middle class but also for the urban interests who own property and who benefit from this consumption. For Coleman, CCTV is a social process that is linked inextricably to an alliance that has emerged within urban governance between the neoliberal local state and business interests. In his view, an understanding of the state and the material interests that shape it is pivotal if one is adequately to explain urban social control strategies such as CCTV. The core point here is that the state, social control and social order need to be considered in terms of a series of relationships and interconnections. Coleman (2004: 33) argues that 'neoliberal rule is articulated in and through dominant social bodies and networks of state power', and technologies such as CCTV operate in the economic interests of this 'ruling social bloc'. In his view, the state seeks to maintain social order as a strategy (overt or otherwise) for maintaining the (capitalist) social order. In other words, CCTV is much more than simply a technology for urban crime prevention.

In a similar vein, Keith Hayward (2004) aims to bring an understanding of the city and the urban experience to the analysis of urban crime. He starts from the premise that the routines, rhythms and spatial manifestations of everyday urban life and their intersections with consumerism that pervade contemporary society are implicated in the conduct, nature, extent and definition of crime. Where Hayward diverges from most attempts to explain the link between urban criminal activity and the contexts within which it occurs is that his starting point is the city and urban and social theory, not crime and criminology. In Hayward's view, a more robust understanding of the relationship between people and their cities, cultures and societies is needed. At the core of this relationship, he argues, is consumption, which is reshaping urban space by day and night, including the location and nature of commercial, residential and leisure places and the ways in which these spaces are used (and, indeed, policed): '[C]onsumer culture and its associated practices are . . . contributing to the *substantial spatial and situational reconfiguration of the post-industrial city*' (Hayward 2004: 11).

Also altered, in Hayward's view, are the emotions and desires which underpin contemporary urban life and, by extension, much criminal activity. His point is that in order to understand urban crime and disorder it is necessary first to understand the social, spatial and cultural conditions that fostered it. Hayward further argues that it is necessary to grasp the emotional and lived dimensions of urban crime, as these, too, are often embedded in urban consumer culture (see also Chapter 5). In this view, desire and fear intersect to shape the contemporary criminal landscape, with the dominant urban culture of consumerism fostering in some a desire for the goods and lifestyles from which they are (materially and often physically) excluded. Hayward goes on to suggest that it is this longing that underpins many new forms of criminal behaviour at the same time as the fear of crime and the 'other' is leading to greater spatial segregation as well as prompting calls for increased surveillance and policing. The distinction that was developed by cultural theorist Michel de Certeau (1988/1980) between the 'concept' or rational city of planning and theory and the lived city of experience serves as a theoretical touchstone for this argument. But the issue is broader than this, extending to the nature of marginality and the factors that differentially position people, positively and negatively, in the city and particularly in the city at night.

## Marginality and the urban night

Diversity is often cited as being at the heart of 'successful' after-dark cities and urban spaces (see Chapter 3). But the city at night is also a space of urban subcultures, many of which are outside official discourses of 'acceptable' diversity. Indeed, darkness facilitates the 'counter-hegemonic practices' of many otherwise 'marginalized groups' (Williams 2008: 520). Practices such as 'rave parties', drug use and trading, and prostitution are often named in this context, being also often discussed as instances of resistance to authority and empowering expressions of identity. The forms of surveillance discussed above and the implementation of a range of formal and informal strategies, including regulation and building defensive forms of architecture, gentrification and, indeed, fostering the development of the night-time economy itself, should all be understood in the context of seeking to control and spatially either to contain the activities of groups that fall outside the mainstream or shield sections of society from the possibility of coming into contact with them. The night-time is also the space of the homeless, who seek refuge in public spaces, such as doorways and parks. It is the time when this group is both most visible and most vulnerable.

*[margin handwriting: homeless highly visible.]*

As discussed above, many urban precincts at night are monocultural in terms of their use and the demographic profile of their users. Similarly, many precincts become abandoned once shops and businesses have closed. These factors are causes of considerable concern to local authorities and residents alike. But as they seek to address them, important questions have emerged relating to the marginalization and exclusion of particular groups from the night-time economy which have occurred often as a direct result of government policy and regulation. Indeed, even in the context of increased private policing and electronic surveillance, many people's perceptions and use of the city after dark are curtailed or moulded by fear and apprehension – fear of violent crime, unease about strangers, and feeling marginalized by the types of activities that dominate a space. In the city of the night, 'fear centres on the presence and behaviour of others' (Pain and Townshend 2002: 105). Class, ethnicity and age are key structuring elements shaping marginalization and fearfulness (Talbot 2011), as are sexuality and gender (Chatterton and Hollands 2003; Tomsen and Markwell 2007), while Gill Valentine et al. (2010) have traced the role that the dominance of alcohol plays in marginalizing many Muslims from the spaces of the night-time economy in British cities. Such social fault-lines in different ways shape how the night-time city is used, experienced and imagined and, although often conceived in terms of discourses of inclusion and nurturing the public realm, night-time economies have formed as sites of exclusion that are 'symptomatic of existing social, economic and cultural divisions where not only new segregations are defined but also older inequalities are reinforced' (Brabazon and Mallinder 2007: 172).

*[margin handwriting: fear-fulness]*

One must be wary of simplifying and generalizing women's engagement with the city. According to Elizabeth Wilson (1992: 6), for instance: 'Woman is present in cities as tempt-

*[margin handwriting: women's perspective experience]*

ress, as whore, as fallen woman, as lesbian, but also as virtuous womanhood in danger, as heroic womanhood who triumphs over temptation and tribulation.' Nevertheless, it is well established that fear of physical violence and assault is an important dimension leading many women to avoid, if not the city at night, then certain spaces within it at particular times. Women carefully map their movement through urban space, being drawn at night to those places that are well lit and populated and avoiding the dark and deserted. The following rather evocative passage from the official American website of Take Back the Night is illustrative of the way in which many women experience even familiar urban space after dark:

> A woman walks alone down a dark, deserted street. With every shadow she sees, and every sound she hears, her pounding heart flutters and skips a beat. She hurries her pace as she sees her destination become closer. She is almost there. She reaches the front door, goes inside, collects herself, and moves on forgetting, at least for tonight, the gripping fear that momentarily enveloped her life. (Take Back the Night website, http://www.takebackthenight.org/history.html, accessed April 2012)

The threat here is both imagined, material and lived. There is, for instance, strong evidence suggesting that women are much less likely to be the victims of crime in the urban nighttime than are young men (Thomas and Bromley 2000). But where (young, heterosexual) men may feel invincible in the night city irrespective of its dangers, women are likely to feel vulnerable. Almost every study of perceptions of urban safety confirms that women are more fearful than men of becoming the victim of violent urban crime (Pain 2001; Valentine 1989), a finding that is regarded by many feminists as both evidence and outcome of patriarchy and the structural subordination of women in society. The Islington Crime Surveys conducted in the 1980s by a team of criminologists in the United Kingdom are much cited in the literature on women's fear in urban space. It was found that 73 per cent of women compared with 27 per cent of men were concerned about going out alone at night, and 68 per cent of women aged under twenty-five 'took some form of avoidance action at night through fear of crime, avoiding certain streets, carrying items that could be used as weapons of self-defence. Some 43 per cent of women claimed to avoid public transport at night for fear of crime' (Worpole 1992: 52). Similarly, the British Crime Survey, which was conducted between 1981 and 1995, found that in response to the question, 'How safe do you feel walking alone in the street after dark?' 47 per cent of women and only 15 per cent of men said that they experienced some degree of fear in this situation, while 33 per cent of women admitted to a fear of being raped (Thomas and Bromley 2000: 1410). It is well established that women manage their presence and use of the city at night in ways intended to reduce their risk of becoming the victims of crime. This management relates not only to their movement through public space, but also to the clubs and bars they frequent when participating in the night-time economy and the way in which they use and claim these spaces, with many managing their presence by marking out and sustaining a 'space of privacy' within a venue (Waitt et al. 2011).

Rachel Pain (2001) suggests that research into women's fear in, and of, urban space pivots on two central paradoxes. The first is the apparent discrepancy that exists between the levels of women's fear of crime and the official (reported) levels of violence against them. Feminists, however, have challenged this 'vulnerability paradox' and argued that the impression of a mismatch is an outcome of the difference between the real and the perceived which lies not in the relative absence of incidents of violence against women, but in the narrow way in which crimes against women are defined and crime statistics gathered. Research utilizing different ('more sensitive') ways of categorizing and understanding violence against women in urban space reveals that the rates are much higher than is usually thought, which suggests that women's levels of fear are, in fact, justified (Pain 2001: 903). The second paradox underpinning the research into women's fear of violence in urban space, according to Pain, is the clear discrepancy between the strength of this fear compared with their lack of fear of those spaces where they are most likely to be the victims of violence – in the private realm. In other words, women are safer (statistically at least) in public space than they are in their homes, but, in Pain's view, because society places a high value on the institution of the family and the space of the private home, women rarely think that this is the case. Pain also points to the limitations of attempts to use urban planning and design to reduce women's fear of public space whilst ignoring the social and cultural factors that underpin it.

Survey data notwithstanding, it is also well established that different women fear urban space in different ways, with age and class being perhaps the most significant variables (Thomas and Bromley 2000). Where older and/or middle-class women's use of urban space in the day and night may be curtailed by the fear of being the victim of a violent crime, younger women are not necessarily as inhibited (Pain 2001). Indeed, the evidence is mounting that for many young women urban space at night is a site of pleasure, opportunity and adventure, as well as of danger and uncertainty. This is a presence, however, that is also cut through with contradictions. The city can offer women the freedom to transgress. But their presence in the city at night historically has been considered a 'problem of order', in part because of its symbolic association with 'the promise of sexual adventure' (Wilson 1992: 6). As a result, much urban and social policy has been underpinned by the aim of controlling/containing women's movement through the night-time city. Lefebvre's notion of the 'right to the city' can perhaps be recast as 'women's right to the carnival, intensity and even the risks of the city' (Wilson 1992: 10) – the right to be disorderly. Under conditions of the night-time economy, young women are present in ever-increasing numbers in much-maligned alco-centric leisure precincts and many are embracing the so-called 'carnivalesque' of this socio-temporal space with considerable relish.

The emergence of the stimulation approach to the night-time economy coincided with a number of significant social changes which meant that women had much greater capacity to partake in leisure and consumption than was previously the case. Of importance are increases in their participation in the workforce, leisure time, the age of marriage and child rearing, and discretionary income (Chatterton and Hollands 2003: 154). Also important, though, have been changes to the structure and expression of women's friendships and the associated patterns of socializing, including a marked increase in so-called 'ladies' nights out' and the institutionalization of 'hen nights', which often involve male strippers and other inversions of gender roles and stereotypes (Wearing et al. 2010). Women's use of the city at night has thus grown exponentially with the development of leisure-focused night-time economy strategies (Jayne et al. 2011). Indeed, women are often explicitly targeted by the night leisure industry, and to this end there has been an increase in 'female-friendly' venues and an associated decline in traditional male-dominated pubs and bars (Chatterton and Hollands 2003). While increased freedom in the night-time city may be considered evidence of gender-based leisure 'equality', Paul Chatterton and Robert Hollands (2003: 148) suggest that it 'has often been on male terms, and contains . . . negative consequences like increased levels of drunkenness, violence and drug consumption'. In other words, young women are behaving in the city at night in very similar ways to young men. And the result has been something of a moral panic prompted largely by the incongruity of established notions of femininity and those of the drunken female body in public space (Waitt et al. 2011). It becomes once again a question of order.

*[handwritten margin note: women participating in city life in a traditionally 'male' terms.]*

At different times in Australia and the United Kingdom, government-funded media campaigns have been run in an attempt to address the problem of 'binge drinking' that has become such a feature of the night-time economy, and women have explicitly been targeted. The aim, in effect, is to tell young women what is appropriate behaviour in the urban night-time economy. Central to these campaigns has been what Rebecca Brown and Melissa Gregg (forthcoming) call a 'pedagogy of regret', whereby intoxicated young women are depicted in a range of vulnerable, degrading and often sexually compromising situations in the urban night-time as an outcome of being drunk. Regret is used as a tactic intended to scare young women into controlling their behaviour and protecting themselves from doing something they will later 'regret'. The advertisements play on well-established fears about the dangers that lurk for women in the city at night, including the risk of rape and sexual assault, but it is also assumed/hoped that the target audience will regard both the depicted behaviour and its consequences as undesirable.

Underpinning this expectation are 'ideals of normative femininity and heterosexuality, in which young women strive to appear "respectable"' (Brown and Gregg forthcoming). As Brown and Gregg (forthcoming) and Gordon Waitt et al. (2011) argue, however, rather than being sources of regret 'in the morning', the empirical evidence suggests that, for many young women, excessive drinking and disorderly behaviour whilst drunk are actually important aspects of their enjoyment of a night out. Indeed, this enjoyment may actually be heightened by the sharing of anecdotes and images afterwards, usually via social media such as Facebook. It may be, too, that drinking and drunkenness are key elements of the way in which many young women now express their friendships and assert their feminine identities (Waitt et al. 2011).

*[handwritten margin note: drinking as key element to friendships & ways to assert feminine identities.]*

## Conclusion

The city at night has long been regarded as a turbulent space of transgression and danger. It is also a space that is frequently overlooked by urban theorists and urban planners alike. If the concept of the city has a temporal code, it is unequivocally that of the day. Since the 1970s, however, both the problems and potential of the city after dark have increasingly become the objects of scrutiny as changes to the nature of work and leisure have also changed the ways in which cities are used. In response, many cities focused considerable resources on trying to invigorate themselves at night in order to address the spatial and economic consequences of both temporality and decline. Strategies adopted have included gentrification, time-shifting, changing the liquor licensing regulations to support late-night entertainment venues, and generally trying to foster the leisure and cultural industries. While the aim of these strategies is economic growth and the enlivenment of the city centre, the result has frequently been the creation of monocultural urban night-time economies focused on the consumption of alcohol. This landscape is one of excess, crime and public disorder.

This chapter examined both the stimulation approach to the urban night-time economy and resulting attempts to address the problems this approach, in part, creates. Central here is a strong law and order focus, which has led to increased surveillance and policing. There have also been attempts to use spatial containment as a tactic either through curfews and lockouts or by clearly demarcating late-night drinking precincts. These approaches have had limited success and most fail to address the social and cultural factors that are at the core of the changing nature of leisure and consumption. Gender provides a fascinating lens through which to consider some of these issues because the relationship between women and the city at night is multifaceted and, frequently, contradictory. For some women the city after dark is a place of potential danger, while for others it is a site of pleasure and empowerment. What is clear, however, is that the night-time economy is a complex phenomenon requiring a range of interconnecting approaches and an interdisciplinary sensibility if it is to be understood and its challenges are to be addressed. What also emerged from the discussion of the city at night is the place of emotion in the use and experience of urban space, with the emotion of fear being one that recurs. It is the relationship between the city and emotion that is the concern of the next chapter.

how about our BC laws that kick everyone out of the bars at closing at the same time; therefore, putting a big mix of intoxicated people out of the streets together?
→ fighting/assaults.

# 5
# Emotional City

## Memory, Belief and Passion

> The city – as experience, environment, concept – is constructed by means of multiple contrasts: natural, unnatural; monolithic, fragmented; secret, public; pitiless, enveloping; rich, poor; sublime, beautiful.
>
> Wilson 1992: 8

## Introduction

Cities are the spaces of 'multiple contrasts', eliciting a range of emotional responses and engagements that are collective as well as individual. Not only do they contain within them the places of contradiction, memory and experience, sites of fear and intimacy, but, following Wilson above, they are built at the interface of such contradictions and juxtapositions. Urban landscapes can be regarded as inspirational and poignant in both their beauty and their degradation. Indeed, it is such responses that art and architecture, in different ways, often seek to evoke, engage with and comment on. The relationship between cities, built space and emotions is complex and little understood within urban studies. Emotions inhabit and gain shape in the micro spaces of the everyday. Similarly, systems of identity, meaning and belonging which are socially produced and constituted are also central to the symbolic and physical delineation of place. The starting point for this chapter is an acknowledgement that cities and urban life cannot be understood fully in the absence of some consideration of the structures and rhythms not just of meaning but also of emotion that are embedded in the concept of place. It is the resulting approaches to conceptualizing the city that are probed in this chapter.

The chapter begins by tracing a sociological understanding of the emotions that makes it possible to explain their importance in shaping people's engagement with the city and urban space without slipping into either psychologism or constructivism. The chapter goes on to consider the spaces of memory and memorial and their connections to the experience and expression of emotion and meaning. Such outpouring occurs formally through monuments, statues and shrines, but also informally through everyday rituals and practices. Built structures such as cemeteries and monuments are intended to stimulate certain emotional responses as well as be markers of place and collective identity. The final section of the chapter examines the role of religion and belief in city building – a link that can be traced back to the earliest days of the city.

## Emotions in place

Cities and urban space evoke a complex of emotional responses that are grounded in diverse patterns and biographies of use, experience and imagination, and informed by a range of social and cultural factors. Fear, for instance, plays an important, albeit often insidious, role in structuring women's use of the city, particularly at night (see Chapter 4), while the notion of 'home' is highly evocative and yet deceptively simple. Nevertheless, the affective is invariably overlooked or dismissed in urban sociological accounts focused on macro structures and processes. What potentially go unexamined as a result are significant intersections, nuances and consequences. Not only do cities summon the emotions, but the emotional – the so-called 'sector of spontaneity and passion' (Lefebvre 2008a/1961: 141) – is an important intangible dimension of the spatial structuring of society, which is, in part, informed by the interconnected configurations of meaning that are the outcome of individual and shared relationships to, and perceptions and experiences of, place – what Raymond Williams (1961) calls 'structures of feeling'.

Jack Barbalet (1998: 9) suggests that while most sociologists are comfortable with frameworks conceptualizing the emotions as social constructs, they are frequently uneasy with the proposition that 'social relationships, institutions and processes' are themselves shaped in some way by the emotions. In Barbalet's (2002: 2) view, however, this hesitancy must be overcome because there can be no action in any society 'without emotional involvement'. Therefore, attempting to understand the relationship between the emotions and social action is an important task for sociology and not least for its urban sub-discipline and more broadly for urban studies. Emotions that are experienced in response to circumstances or encounters with others, including, I would add, with the spatial and the non-human, motivate and enable action. Thus emotion connects structure and agency, and its study can provide insights into this connection as well as into the dynamic simultaneity that is the macro and the micro, the city as material, imagined and lived. What is required is an approach that works with and against the grain of each without reducing one to the other or assuming a predictable, unidirectional relationship of cause and effect. In other words, the starting point must be to accept not only that social and spatial processes are meaningful and shape emotions, but also that the emotional realm influences society and its spatiality, including their intersections in cities and everyday urban life. This is not to argue that emotions make people act in certain preordained ways. On the contrary, the point is that the lived experience of emotion 'inclines' or predisposes them to action. The resulting actions may conform to well-established rhythms or patterns and thus be unsurprising, but regularity and, indeed, a level of likelihood should not be mistaken for determination or inevitability.

Just as emotions experienced in response to particular social situations do not elicit predictable (re)actions, it is also mistaken to suggest that urban space causes certain types of behaviour or triggers a given set of emotional responses. Similarly, space should not be regarded as the inert context within which free-floating feelings are expressed and (re)actions played out. Rather, cities and urban space evoke emotions, and these emotions, in turn, influence place-based social action. There may be cultural or deeply idiosyncratic factors at play, but feelings about place are implicated, as facilitators, in a range of collective and individual actions. Place, and the sentiments it arouses, can influence the way in which people act in relation to a specific place and in their dealings with others. Fear, as mentioned above, can be a powerful motivator shaping how space is both used and regarded. Similarly, urban social movements are frequently emotionally charged responses to the prospect of urban change, while activities within the property market can be strongly influenced by emotion. For instance, as any real estate agent will attest, the act of buying or selling a 'home', whilst having important and indisputable cultural and economic dimensions, is also laden with emotional significance – memory and sentiment, perhaps grief and nostalgia. Moreover, the emotional stress that comes from buying or selling a home is also widely acknowledged, and many contemporary rites of passage are framed through the emotionally charged practices and processes of home ownership. It has also become increasingly evident that emotional engagements with place are implicated in the construction of social and personal identities, with space being a pivotal factor in the constitution of the subject. People identify individually and collectively with where they live, with a particular house, in a particular street, in a particular neighbourhood, town, city or region (Urry 1985). These locations are imbued with cultural and personal meaning and also have the ability to arouse often very powerful emotions, including feelings of security, love and belonging, alienation, hatred and dread.

Henri Lefebvre (2008a/1961), in seeking to focus attention on the 'moments' of everyday life and the need for sociology to engage with the coexistence of place-based social and physiological rhythms, argued that the physiological influences the social, just as the social moulds the physiological. But, importantly, rather than focusing on theorizing the emotions *per se*, he sought to proffer the methodological point that 'making sense of a city requires an emotional lens' (Bruno 2002: 384). This is, in part, what Lefebvre's theory of moments was about, and, as discussed in Chapter 1, mapping the parameters of such an approach was a task of his rhythmanalysis project.

*Simmel* →

Georg Simmel, in his influential 1903 essay 'The Metropolis and Mental Life', was one of the first sociologists to take seriously the relationship between the city and the emotional. Indeed, emotions, according to Simmel (1995: 31), are at the very core of metropolitan life and the forming of the 'metropolitan type': 'The psychological foundation, upon which the metropolitan individuality is erected, is the intensification of emotional life due to the swift and continuous shift of external and internal stimuli.' Simmel argues that everyday life in the modern city is one of sensory bombardment, where 'violent stimuli' accompany 'every crossing of the street'. The city is the site of movement, circulation and frenetic rhythms. The metropolis is also defined by networks and associations that are complex, impersonal, intersecting and hierarchical, and thus responding emotionally to every person and situation encountered in the course of a day would bring on an 'unthinkable mental condition' (Simmel 1995: 37). The city dweller is thus impelled either to suffer or to adapt. So in order to cope with daily city life and its high level of sensory confusion, he or she has developed a disposition which is instrumental, blasé and reserved, and resides in 'buildings and in educational institutions, in the wonders and comforts of space-conquering techniques, in the formations of social life, and in the concrete institutions of the State' (Simmel 1995: 44).

The development of a specific metropolitan temperament is thus a 'strategy for self-preservation' (Frisby 2007: 153), a seemingly rational and intellectualized response to the amplification of emotional life. In contrast, the rhythm, pace and psychological and emotional consequences of everyday life in the small town are supposedly very different. The non-urban resident does not have to deal with heightened levels of sensory bombardment but instead has a mental life that 'rest[s] more on feelings and the emotional' (Simmel 1995: 31). Simmel (1995: 31) argues that he or she is able to engage fully with day-to-day encounters because these are familiar and predictable, having gentle rhythms that are 'rooted in the unconscious levels of the mind'. The small town is a

*vs. Simple living in small towns.*

space where the emotional thrives 'in the steady equilibrium of unbroken customs'. Simmel's theorization is soundly located in the rural–urban tradition in the study of cities and urban life (see Chapter 6). In contrast, however, to analyses that rested on positioning the city as 'bad', in opposition to the country as 'good', Simmel's assessment of the urban is far more complex and certainly not negative. Rather, he sees the city as providing a space for levels of freedom and the toleration of difference that does not exist in the intimate communities of the non-urban. It is the customary and the everyday emotional that, according to Simmel, operate to constrain (see Chapter 6). Importantly, too, not only does Simmel's analysis recast the rural–urban, but it also disrupts another influential sociological dualism: the emotional and the rational.

As with the rural and the urban, Simmel's conceptualization of the relationship between emotion and rationality is also highly nuanced (perhaps contradictory), and although he argues that the rational has displaced the emotional as the defining disposition of modernity and the contemporary metropolis, the source of the rational is not the absence of the emotional but, in fact, the presence of the *hyper-*emotional. Put differently, rationality thrives in the context of a particular form of emotional stimulation – the city equals the rational *because* it is the realm of the hyper-emotional not because it transcends it. So while the rational may be said to displace emotion, it does not, according to this perspective, replace it. Indeed, Barbalet (1998: 55) suggests that there is a further level of complexity to Simmel's understanding of the relationship between emotion and the metropolis: 'Simmel's argument is not simply that rational calculability and exactness form a "protective organ" against the disturbingly intense emotional life which would other-wise ensue. It is also that the protective organ of rationality is itself covered with an emotional cloak, what Simmel calls the "blasé outlook" and the "blasé attitude" '. Simmel's approach is significant because although the opposition of the emotional and the rational is commonplace within sociology, this opposition is usually underpinned both by the rejection of the emotional as an appropriate object/level of analysis, and the assumption that rationality is superior to

*[handwritten margin notes: mixes the binaries of rational/emotional & adopts]*

emotion (Barbalet 2002). It is possible to argue that Simmel eschews both rejection and hierarchy and assumes, instead, intersection and a form of interdependency. Barbalet (2002: 1) also rejects the convention of considering the emotions as the 'other' of rationality, saying that 'all actions, and indeed reason itself, require appropriate facilitating emotions if successful actions or reason at all are to be achieved'.

There is also an important gender dimension to the way in which emotion has been viewed within sociology, as men routinely are associated with the rational and the objective – the worlds of progress, work, politics and the economy – while women are linked with the emotional, the superstitious and, thus, the 'irrational' (Grosz 1995). A key objective in rethinking the emotional realm, and, indeed, asserting its importance to understanding the city and the experience of urban space/life, is to claim rationality for women and the emotional for men. It is also to argue that everyday urban life and mundane engagements with urban space are at once emotional *and* rational, male *and* female. So while there may be social and cultural factors shaping emotional responses and patterns that suggest, even reinforce, gender differences, as explained further below, these are neither pre-given nor determined by biology. And it was probably not intended, but in fusing the emotional and the rational and by attaching both to external conditions that are not gendered, Simmel's metropolitan type is by extension both male and female, and the mental life of the metropolis, including its freedoms, is, by further extension, available to, and experienced by, all city dwellers, irrespective of gender. That said, Simmel does not consider gender or the role of gender relationships in shaping the use of urban space and the parameters and experience of metropolitanism, just as he avoids any consideration in his analysis of other important elements of social stratification and urban difference, including class and ethnicity (Frisby 2007: 154).

The question of where the collective fits into sociological understandings of the emotions and the city is clearly a critical one. It is commonplace, for instance, to talk of there being mass public outpourings of grief in response to momentous events, such as the destruction in 2001 of the World Trade Center towers in New York City and the death of

Princess Diana in 1997. Similarly, the collective expression of emotions associated with victory and defeat that is a feature of sporting fandom is well established (Rowe and Baker 2012; Vertinsky and Bale 2004). Such phenomena also have important spatial dimensions – sport fandom, for instance, is frequently connected to an identification with a particular town or city, while major social trauma is routinely marked by built memorials. Collective emotion can be that which is expressed jointly and publicly, or, as Barbalet argues with reference to the fear of unemployment, it can also be social, not simply because it relates to a particular social phenomenon, but because it is 'experienced and shared by members of a social collectivity' (Barbalet 1998: 158). Put differently, collective emotional experience does not necessarily suggest the communal (public) expression of emotion, although it can; rather, a collective emotion can be that which is held in common by a particular social group. People of the same gender, race and class, for instance, may experience similar emotions because of their common situation within the social structure. Their structural equivalence means they may well have had similar life experiences and thus have similar emotional dispositions (Stets and Turner 2008).

5.1 President Obama at the Ground Zero memorial, New York City, USA.

Emotions, therefore, differentiate and demarcate social collectives and can, as discussed above, be a basis for collective action, such as urban protest. This perspective further lifts the study of emotion above the level of the group and the psychological to that of the social and, in Barbalet's view, the distribution of power and status. Barbalet (1998: 159) goes on to suggest that the term 'emotional climate' is useful in this context: 'Emotional climates are sets of emotions or feelings which are not only shared by groups of individuals implicated in common social structures and process, but which are also significant in the formation and maintenance of political and social identities and collective behaviour.' This observation does not mean, of course, that all members of a group will necessarily experience, or act on, the same feelings or sentiments. On the contrary, emotional climates may be shared but 'individual participation in them will be patterned and therefore unequal' (Barbalet 1998: 159). Social groups are comprised of difference as well as commonality, and the processes by which the specific concerns of collectives are created and replicated are the mechanisms whereby frameworks of emotion and meaning are developed and redeveloped. Following John Urry (1985), the spatial is an element in the structuration of the society, thus co-location and shared identification with place can be the basis for the formation of an emotional climate. Places are about relationships. The triggers for emotion are embedded not only in the immediacy of experience but also in memories about, and nostalgia for, place. Thus memory and the spaces of the past can be significant elements of a place-based emotional climate and cause for collective action. Emotions in place and located emotional climates are also comprised of 'traces of the memories of different social groups who have lived in or passed through' a particular locale (Urry 2005: 80).

## Memory and urban space

The proposition that the city is the repository of collective and individual memories points to the status of built memorials and monuments as well as to the unmarked and the unremarkable – the everyday urban landscape. According to Urry (1985: 39), long-established social practices and power relations have cultural forms and patterns that are intergenerationally reproduced through buildings and the urban landscape. The present city is built on the physical layers (remnants) of the cities and settlements that have preceded it as well as on the cultures, social structures, emotions and memories that shaped and are embedded in those layers – tiers of 'historical time superimposed on each other or different architectural strata' (Boyer 1996: 19). As the city enshrines the past, contemporary practices and social relations become incorporated into new environments. The city is thus a store of memory and the bygone as well as of the lived and contemporaneous. Sometimes the layers are evident, but more often they lie beneath the surface awaiting excavation or recollection. M. Christine Boyer (1996), in writing on collective memory and the urban landscape, including its most obvious intersection in the processes of built heritage preservation, highlights the ways in which architecture, planning and the symbolic are constructed and/or configured to represent the city, its past and future. In this context, Boyer (1996: 31) explains the importance of city memory as follows:

> Although the name of a city may remain forever constant, its physical structure constantly evolves, being deformed and forgotten, adapted to other purposes or eradicated by different needs. The demands and pressures of social reality constantly affect the material order of the city, yet it remains the theater of our memory. Its collective forms and private realms tell us of the changes that are taking place; they remind us as well of the traditions that set this city apart from others. It is in these artifacts and traces that our city memories lie buried, for the past is carried forward to the present through these sites.

What is necessary, Boyer argues, is to understand how architecture and planning play with, order and frequently manipulate these traces, both theoretically and in practice. The tendency to historical quotation evident in many so-called 'postmodern' landscapes and buildings is discussed in this context. Postmodern forms of architecture aim to 'speak' simultaneously the fundamentally contradictory languages of tradition and change. They often do this by making playful use of symbolism, ornamentation and historical references intended to invoke the past at the same time as asserting the fashionable and the technologically sophisticated (Harvey 1989a). The result, however, is often pastiche and cliché – the trivialization of memory and historical context. But Boyer (1996: 66) goes on to explain that history occupies the space created when collective memory no longer exists in the living memory of a particular social group. Where collective memory assumes continuity and relevance, history assumes rupture and fragmentation.

Influencing Boyer, and perhaps one of the most important thinkers on the relationship between the city and memory, is the German theorist Walter Benjamin (1973, 1979, 1995). Writing in the first half of the twentieth century, Benjamin conceptualized urban memory as being enmeshed in a complex of connections between individual and collective experiences of urban space as well as cultural traditions and processes (Frisby 2007; Gilloch 1997). Indeed, as Mike Savage and Alan Warde (1993: 123) explain, Benjamin's work 'addressed urban meaning as the interface between personal memories and experiences, and the historical construction of dominant meanings and values'. Central to Benjamin's conceptualization was the intriguing figure of the *flâneur*, who, in the act of strolling the newly constructed arcades of nineteenth-century Paris, did not simply observe urban life but engaged in an 'archaeological' process of unearthing the myths and 'collective dreams' of the city and modernity (Frisby 1986: 224). *Flânerie*, then, is a way of reading or interpreting urban landscapes, a methodology for uncovering the traces of collective memory and social meaning that are embedded in the layered fabric of the city (Stevenson 2003). In other words, the city for Benjamin is the space of 'perception and memory' (Tonkiss 2005: 120) and its interpretation requires a form of deep enthnography.

At the level of individual or personal memory of the city, Benjamin highlights the importance both of the remembrances of childhood relationships with urban space and the need to observe the city anew as if a child. Taking the position of the child supposedly 'creates distance between viewer and viewed, subject and object' (Gilloch 1997: 61), which conversely heightens the clarity with which one sees the city; it makes the viewed more noticeable and defined. This approach, in Graeme Gilloch's opinion, aims to 'dereify' the city and facilitate explanation and criticism. Advocating the need to view the city in the way of a child assumes the playfulness, serendipity, intimacy and naïvety with which children engage with place. Children do not just observe their surroundings but are immersed in them, in part because of their physical size relative to the adult scale of the city, but also because of the embodied nature of their engagement with place and the lucidity of their gaze. As Gilloch (1997: 65) explains, Benjamin, in writing about the remembered city of his own childhood, 'does not 're-seek lost times' in order to generate a space in which description is possible, but instead tries to recapture the lost perspective, the pre-habitual gaze of the child'. Advocating the need to see the city in this way is not an invitation to nostalgia. Indeed, Fran Tonkiss (2005: 121) cautions that 'this is not a straight transcription of events from an earlier life but an act of imagination in the present, just as memory is not a means to access the past but the medium for its experience'.

The city thus is conceptualized as a labyrinth enshrining the traces and fragments of lives, moments and cultural practices as well as buildings and monuments, which can be uncovered ('memorized') through the acts of walking and looking. Benjamin, the archaeologist of the city, was also concerned with its monuments and memorials. These places, including cemeteries and other shrines, are important and highly visible elements of the urban landscape and frame a sense of place and identity, as well as a relationship with time and history. Gilloch (1997: 72) suggests that Benjamin's enduring concern to understand 'the character of the city as it appears in memory (the remembered city) and . . . memory as it appears in the city (urban memory) coalesce in his conceptualization of the monument'.

Urban monuments are markers of victory and social and political power – partial, frequently false, statements of events and historical circumstances. Thus each is to a great extent a 'petrified myth' (Gilloch 1997: 72). Nevertheless, as

Lefebvre (2008b/1981: 132) observes, monuments, resonant with 'memory and symbolism', are 'indispensable to the urban'. He notes in this context that such monuments are features of the city centre and notably absent from the suburbs. Benjamin's focus was on the monuments of the nineteenth century, the statues of rulers, military heroes, victories and the markers of colonialism and empire. The meaning of such statuary may change with time and circumstance, and its removal is frequently a symbolic marker of regime change, as was the case with the statue of Saddam Hussein in central Baghdad, which was physically toppled by invading US troops in April 2003. Benjamin calls for the critical reading of monuments in order to reveal their myths and paradoxes. Feminists have also probed the links between power and the urban, exposing the masculine codes embedded in the built environment, including both the obvious symbolism of city skylines dominated by skyscrapers, as well as the unequal gender relations more subtly inscribed in urban monuments and the design of streetscapes. Janice Monk (1992), for instance, further observes that women are rarely the subjects in their own right of public statues of the type discussed by Benjamin. Rather, statues featuring women tend to represent them either as monarch or as the mythological symbol of lofty ideals such as victory, justice or liberty.

In titling a chapter on the important City Beautiful movement 'The City of Monuments', urban planning historian Peter Hall (1992: 174) draws attention to the empirical reality that urban monumentalism goes beyond statues and built structures to encompass entire urban landscapes and city building trends. The City Beautiful is the name given to an approach to urban design that emerged during the nineteenth century with the radical rebuilding of the central districts of a number of European cities, including Paris and Vienna. The most notable nineteenth-century practitioner associated with this approach was Georges Haussmann, whose reconstruction of Paris under the auspices of Emperor Louis Napoleon III transformed the look and feel of that city from a place of dark and narrow streets to one of grand boulevards, civic buildings and a lively street culture. In addition, the boulevards became places for military parades and symbolic displays of the Emperor's supremacy. As Malcolm

Miles (1997: 23) neatly explains, 'Whilst medieval streets were gaps between buildings, in the Baroque city they became avenues of procession.' The use of the Parisian boulevards for this and other forms of political urban spectacle continued throughout the twentieth century. For instance, during the Second World War the invading Germans used a parade down the Champs Élysées as a way of symbolically claiming the city for the Third Reich (another marker of regime change), while Charles de Gaulle's leading of the parade down the same boulevard to mark the liberation of Paris is an enduring post-war image.

It was in the twentieth century, however, that the City Beautiful movement found its most widespread expression – in particular, in the plans and built form of the major cities of many emerging, often postcolonial, nations, such as India, Australia and the United States, and those of the 'new' totalitarian empires of that century, including the Soviet Union and Nazi Germany (Hall 1992). With the City Beautiful movement the connection between the urban landscape and the power relations that underpin all urban development, monumentalism and civic architecture was made explicit. With differing emphases, it has been power in all its manifestations, including political, religious, economic, military and gender, that singularly or in various combinations has been significant. The spaces of the City Beautiful are those of the civic or public realm – the sites of ceremonies, parades and imposing public architecture, of movement and congregation (see Chapter 3). They are also places in the city centre where large numbers of strangers can mingle in ways not possible in the cramped streets and lane-ways of Renaissance or medieval city centres. In cities around the world, the social relations sustaining the City Beautiful legitimated the design and construction of potent symbols of supremacy in the form of monuments, streetscapes and buildings, and in the location and design of parks and gardens. It is certainly the case that the ideas of the City Beautiful underpinned city building that was monumental in both scale and intent and was influential in enshrining the secular symbolic in the urban environment.

Lewis Mumford suggests that the demarcated ceremonial site that is now an important symbolic element of the modern city actually predates the city. These sites were, he argues, the 'first germ of the city' (Mumford 1989/1961: 10) – the locations around which human settlement developed. Mumford observes that 'cemeteries and shrines' were amongst the earliest of civic institutions, being significant 'ceremonial meeting place[s]' for families and others. As sites imbued with potent collective and personal sentiments, they became the destinations of pilgrimage and the expression of belief: 'Some of the functions and purposes of the city . . . existed in such simple structures long before the complex association of the city had come into existence and refashioned the whole environment to give them sustenance and support' (Mumford 1989/1961: 10). This refashioning of the landscape has involved the building not only of shrines and sites of remembrance but also of churches and places of worship. Cities and the built spaces of religion are deeply entwined – indeed, in the past in the United Kingdom, city status was granted only to those towns in possession of an Anglican cathedral.

## Landscapes of belief

It is perhaps obvious to state that religion and urban space intersect in a range of important ways, including as prompts for meaning and the expression of emotion. Major organized religions, notably the Catholic Church, have vast land holdings in cities across the world, and this ownership of land brings with it considerable economic as well as political and symbolic power. Clothes marking religious affiliation, such as the burkas and headscarves worn by devout Muslim women, are routine aspects of the spectacle of everyday life in the city. Specialist shops and restaurants catering to certain religious groups – kosher and halal outlets come readily to mind – feature in the landscapes of many cities and are often pointed to as evidence of the tolerance of diversity. Some residential neighbourhoods also have higher concentrations of people from specific religious backgrounds than do other areas: for instance, Jewish quarters and ghettoes, which have been much discussed in the sociological literature (see Chapter 2). But perhaps the most highly visible and monumental expressions of religious belief in any city are the places of worship that frequently dominate their skylines. These are not always on a grand scale, of course; many are discreet and neighbourhood-based, providing some of the city's quiet corners, small spaces for religious reflection. In recent years, it has often been the building of places of worship that has exposed a range of tensions within urban (re)development and fractured the façade of tolerance. A particularly fascinating recent case of the intersection of the politics of religion and the politics of place was the (ill-fated) proposal to build a Muslim community centre two blocks from the site of the former World Trade Center in Manhattan.

Mumford (1989/1961: 265) describes how after the fall of the Roman Empire in Europe, the 'cathedrals, churches, monasteries and shrines' of the Church came to dominate settlements large and small. Indeed, the Church had based its diocesan borders on those of Roman cities (Pirenne 2000: 39). The largest churches with their towering spires and situation in narrow streets were designed to draw the eye upwards – towards heaven. The city, its streets and public spaces, was the location for many of the ceremonial processions and rituals of the Church. The physical spaces of the church, such as St Peter's Basilica in Vatican City, can also be the objects of pilgrimage, while organized religions have long encouraged pilgrims to visit sites of religious significance. Indeed, Donald McNeill (2012) cheekily suggests that in promoting pilgrimages, the Catholic Church was perhaps the 'world's first travel agent'. The 'main purpose' of the medieval European city, as Mumford (1989/1961: 257) explains it, 'was the living of a Christian life', and to this end the structures and institutions of the Church shaped community life in these fledgeling cities:

> [E]ven at its humblest level in the city parish the church was a neighborhood center, a focus of the daily community life; and no neighborhood was so poor that it lacked such a church, even though at the center of the town there might be a vast cathedral big enough to enclose all its citizens on solemn festive occasions. (Mumford 1989/1961: 266–7)

5.2   St Peter's Basilica, Vatican City.

This was a 'world . . . inhabited, haunted by the Church' (Lefebvre 1991/1974: 255). Lefebvre (1991/1974), recognizing the significance of religion to the production of space, brackets it with the political (politico-religious) as a core element of the character of 'absolute space' (see Chapter 1). A key point is that with the Renaissance in Europe from the fourteenth century, the 'representation of space' (the conceived space of scientists, planners, technocrats, and the like) slowly came to dominate the 'representational space' of lived images and symbols, including most notably those 'of religious origin' (Lefebvre 1991/1974: 41). Although absolute space fractured with the rise of secularism (Lefebvre 1991/1974: 256), representational space did not disappear, nor does it survive only in churches and monuments. Rather, Lefebvre (1991/1974: 42) argues that representational space 'is alive: it speaks as an affective kernel or centre: Ego, bed, bedroom, dwelling, house; or: square, church, graveyard. It embraces the loci of passion, of action and of lived situations, and thus immediately implies time . . . it is essentially qualitative, fluid and dynamic.' Space is experienced as real and imagined – 'in the temple, in the city, in the monuments and palaces, the imaginary is transformed into the real' (Lefebvre 1991/1974: 251). It is necessary, therefore, according to Lefebvre, for the study of space to engage both with its origins in history and with its history of representation.

When sociologists seek to understand religion as a social institution, their starting point is often the notion of the sacred and its status in opposition to the profane. Indeed, this is a distinction that has its roots in the work of Émile Durkheim, whose *The Elementary Forms of Religious Life* (1995/1912) is one of the most influential texts in the discipline. For Durkheim, the sacred is the 'extraordinary, that which is set apart from and "above and beyond" the everyday world' (Appelrouth and Edles 2008: 128). This realm is affirmed and produced through shared symbols and rituals – everyday sacred 'moments', which often have spatial dimensions – 'sacred sites (churches, mosques, synagogues) differentiate 'routine' places from those that compel attitudes of awe and inspiration' (Appelrouth and Edles 2008: 129). Max Weber also made an important contribution to the study of religion and religious belief, probing in part the relationship between the city (as ideal-type) and religion. But where Durkheim cast his enquiring gaze on the 'simplest', 'primitive' forms of religion and religious expression, Weber concentrated on the great religions of the world – Christianity, Islam and Judaism – drawing attention, in particular, to the 'specific nature and effects of faith' (Lukes 1981: 457). Weber's ideal city – the medieval guild city – was where religious activity and economic enterprise combined to foster a recognizable urban community. The city, for Weber, played a central part in the development of formal religion. It was

> the basis of specific religious institutions. Not only was Judaism, in contrast with the religion of Israel, a thoroughly urban construction ... but early Christianity is also a city phenomenon; the larger the city the greater was the percentage of Christians, and the case of Puritanism and Pietism was also the same. ... Finally, the city alone produced theological thought, and on the other hand again, it alone harboured thought untrammelled by priestcraft. (Weber 1950/1927: 317)

Weber's analysis rests on the distinction between occidental and oriental cities (as ideal-types). Such dichotomies, their underpinning assumptions and the premise that it is possible to divide the world of cities in this way are now usually regarded as unsustainable. Also unsustainable are labels such as 'Islamic city', 'Christian city' and 'Jewish city'. Janet Abu-Lughod (1987: 155), for instance, asserts that the notion of the Islamic city was constructed by Western authorities drawing upon each other's ideas as well as on 'a small and eccentric sample of pre-modern Arab cities on the eve of Westernization (domination)'. From her tracing of these influences and interrelationships, she argues that cities need to be understood not as religious products, but in terms of the processes that intersected to form them, some of which may, indeed, be religious. For, as discussed above, there are often very important religious influences shaping urban form, both of whole cities and of parts thereof. To this end, Abu-Lughod (1987: 172) identifies the elements which 'set in motion the processes that give rise to Islamic cities'. These factors are: '(1) juridical distinctions between Muslims and/or citizens and outsiders; (2) segregation by gender and a virtually complete division of labor according to it; (3) a fully decentralized and ex post facto system of land use and governmental regulation over space'.

While these three elements are 'Islamic per se', the resulting city form(s) is shaped by a complex of non-Islamic factors, including terrain, climate, history and geography, which connect in time and place with Islamic, as well as prevailing economic, political and social, circumstances and relations. Underpinning much of the discussion about the existence or otherwise of a definitive 'Islamic city' – cities the formation of which is deeply linked to religious processes and power, however contextualized – is an implicit contrast with what are frequently regarded as the non-religious (secular) cities of the West. Western cities came to maturity in the context of modernity and the Enlightenment – the assumption being, following Mumford, Weber and others, that where once religion was a central force in shaping Western cities (and vice versa), this is no longer the case, because with the Enlightenment came the uncoupling of church and state and a weakening of the influence of religion.

This perspective is important to understanding the city not only from the position that the great religions are effectively urban in their character, but also because these religions are deeply entrenched in the urban landscape. Weber's sociology is again important.

The Weberian notion of secularization refers to the process whereby from the sixteenth century onwards more and more spheres of society in the West eschewed explanations grounded in religion and superstition in favour of those based on observable experience, science and the application of reason. This is what is regarded as the triumph of rationality, which resulted in the marginalization of religion (and, as argued in Chapter 5, the affective) and the erosion of the authority of priests and other religious personnel. Frank J. Lechner (1991: 1104) usefully summarizes the core features of secularization as follows:

> Specifically, where official churches used to control substantial economic resources, the relative wealth and capital of these churches has declined; where authority was once legitimated mainly in religious terms and major political conflicts crucially involved religious motives, bureaucratized states now exercise rational-legal authority and separate civil and ecclesiastical spheres; where full membership in the societal community used to depend on one's religious identity and religiously motivated exclusiveness was common, inclusion on the basis of citizenship has transformed the meaning of membership; where religious institutions and elites maintained clear standards of transcendent belief relevant to all spheres of cultural activity, these institutions have lost their hold on the definition of the societal situation, and science, art, and morality no longer require any religious grounding.

The secularization thesis thus implies the separation of church and state – the retreat (or jettisoning) of religion from the public sphere, which is a principle that came to underpin the organization of democratic governments. At its most extreme, however, secularization assumes the disappearance of religion from both the public *and* private spheres (Stevenson et al. 2010). The secular quickly became code for the modern and vice versa, and, following Simmel, the (Western) city came to be regarded as the space that is at the forefront of modernization and hence secularization. In 1965, at the height of modernism, Harvey Cox (1965: 3) confidently claimed:

> This is the age of the secular city. Through supersonic travel and instantaneous communications its ethos is spreading into every corner of the globe. The world looks less and less to religious rules and rituals for its morality or its meanings. For some, religion provides a hobby, for others a mark of national or ethnic identification, for still others an aesthetic delight. For fewer and fewer does it provide an inclusive and commanding system of personal and cosmic values and explanations.

As discussed in Chapter 1, recent theorizing within social science more broadly has called into question the legitimacy of overarching, ethnocentric 'theories of everything', including the secularization thesis. While there may continue to be agreement that aspects of secularization are indeed important features of contemporary urban society, there is general acceptance that assertions regarding the triumph of secularization need to be tempered in the face of credible evidence suggesting, if not contradictory processes, then certainly complexity and multiplicity. There are also questions regarding the relevance of the secularization thesis to non-Christian societies such as China and India, and it is very difficult to argue that secularization is occurring in many Islamic nations, where even in officially secular Turkey the pressure towards desecularization is clearly evident. Elsewhere, in the secular West, the building of mosques and Islamic religious spaces is occurring apace, albeit rarely without controversy (Stevenson et al. 2010). Also challenging the secularization thesis is empirical evidence showing that, unlike the situation in Europe, the proportion of the population of the United States who are religious has remained large and constant for more than sixty years (Habermas 2006). Religiosity also permeates the public sphere in the United States in ways not evident in other Western nations. Indeed, such factors prompt many to argue that Western cities and nations are experiencing simultaneous processes of secularization and desecularization, a combination often described as 'postsecularization' (Habermas 2006), and with this thesis has come research focused on the concept of the 'postsecular city'.

Some have attempted to conceptualize the notion of the postsecular city by investigating the growth of urban faith-based community welfare organizations (Beaumont 2008; Beaumont and Dias 2008). It is well established, for instance, that as a consequence of the growth of neoliberalism in the West and the winding back of the state, primary responsibility for many areas of social welfare and human services has shifted from the public to the private sectors, and specifically to community and religious organizations (Everingham 2003) – key institutions of what David Cameron's British Conservative Party might call the 'Big Society'. With this shift, many faith-based organizations increased their charitable activities and the levels of support they provide to underprivileged groups in the city. David A. Roozen (2009) argues, for instance, that there is a positive correlation between the strength of a religious congregation and the extent of their welfare and volunteering activities.

There are global and national factors at play in shaping the competing processes of postsecularization (including neoliberalism and the retreat from the welfare state), but there are also some very city-specific patterns to the ways in which these processes are expressed. This was highlighted in recent research examining the spatial patterning of religious belief and non-belief across Sydney, Australia, which identified at least five geographies of faith and non-belief (Stevenson et al. 2010). A decrease in Christianity in some parts of the city was matched by an increase in non-Christian faiths, but in other areas there had been little or no change. Perhaps not surprisingly, those areas of the city with considerable affluence, diversity and 'cosmopolitanism' exhibited the highest levels of secularization – what might be termed the retreat from faith. So while the postsecularization thesis acknowledges that the trends are internationally uneven, this research found that they are also highly irregular within individual cities. Such variations reflect very specific city-based factors, including historical and contemporary patterns of immigrant settlement, established and emerging religious groupings, the spatial patterning of class, affluence and gentrification, and the development of zones of cosmopolitanism.

## Conclusion

The conceptualizations of the city that were considered in this chapter are those relating to the themes of emotion, belief and memory, sentiments that are held both collectively and at the level of the individual. What makes them the concern of urban studies is their relationship with cities and urban processes and the ways in which they shape the city as real, imagined and lived. Emotion, for instance, is often overlooked because it is thought to operate at the non-sociological level of irrationality and psychology. This chapter, however, traced the contours of macro-sociological understandings of emotions to reveal its relevance to understanding the urban and attachments to place. The key here is to acknowledge that structures, processes and institutions that are social shape, and are shaped by, emotions. Emotions underpin and facilitate action. Thus the chapter argued that cities and their spaces arouse emotions that, in turn, influence place-based social action and foster a sense of place. The chapter also explained that cities are a series of relationships and the emotions they prompt are as much embedded in memory and the past as they are in the present.

The urban landscape is one of formal and informal memorials, monuments and the markers of memory which are established in the context of emotion and serve as prompts for its expression. Such places are deeply connected with the structures of tradition and the social relations and events which produce cities and urban space. They speak to the texture of the lived city as well as to the social relations and values that shaped it. Important here are the churches and places of worship that frequently dominate cityspace and are markers of the pivotal role of religion to the development of the city. The spaces of belief (built or proposed) are also the spaces of the expression of emotion as well as of power. Religion can be, and is, at the centre of struggles over space, its uses and meanings, while the patterning of religious belief across urban space is often uneven, being the outcome of a complex of factors that operate at a number of levels, including the local and the global. And it is the themes of the global and the local and the enmeshment of cities in multi-scalar networks that are the concerns of the next chapter.

# 6

# Global City

## Hierarchies and the Urban 'Other'

> The main definitions of the city have only one element in common: namely that the city consists simply of a collection of one or more separate dwellings but is a relatively closed settlement.
>
> Weber 1958/1921: 65

## Introduction

Cities and their economies are now increasingly enmeshed in a set of global processes comprised of transnational flows and complex circuits of capital, people, ideas and services that are facilitated by the technologies of media and communication. The global economy is also highly urbanized. It is made up of cities, the links between cities, and shaped by the work that takes place within cities. With increased globalization has come both a fascination with its contours and contradictions as well as the emergence of concerns about the situation of different cities within and outside influential networks. Globalization and, by implication, the associated global hierarchies of cities are founded on notions of a core and a marginalized periphery. The result is the establishment of the context within which cities assertively compete with each other for the status of being ranked (or ranked more highly) with reference to a range of indicators on increasingly influential urban league tables.

The starting point for this chapter is the idea of globalization and its role in processes of urbanization and urban rankings. Central here are the concepts and empirical entities of 'world' and 'global' cities. The chapter considers whether globalization creates homogeneity, as some have argued, or, as is more likely the case, fosters increased heterogeneity and, indeed, hybridity. It is necessary, therefore, to understand the relationship between the global and the local, and the local as it operates under conditions of globalization. The chapter suggests that the existence of global hierarchies of cities, and of cities that appear to transcend the local and national, raises the question of how to understand those cities that seem to fall outside understandings of the urban that have been framed by the global. These are the second cities, the provincial cities and the megacities of the developing South. Also important is the argument that not only do global process and hierarchies define the parameters of the urban, but also they are embedded in theories, assumptions and experiences that are themselves located and shaped by this location. The local is clearly important, but also relevant is an associated revival of interest in the shape and experience of urban community.

## Globalization, networks and circuits

The speed with which the concept of globalization has gained currency in popular and specialist parlance since the 1980s has been truly remarkable. Indeed, writing about globalization in another context, the sociologist David Rowe (2011: 144) reports on the results of his replication of the search of the US Library of Congress for books with the word 'globalization' in the title that was first undertaken by Malcolm Waters in 1994. Where Waters found only thirty-four titles containing globalization or a 'derivative' of the term, Rowe's 'exact wording' search seventeen years later found 5,200, while an associated Google search returned close to twenty-eight million results. Reflecting on these results and the scale of the difference between them, Rowe makes the following points:

> It is not particularly original to observe that the idea of the global has proliferated as an exemplification of itself, flowing across increasingly permeable boundaries and eroding differences – here conceptual and discursive – in all the spaces that it enters. But, inevitably, with all this pervasiveness comes both the elaboration and loss of meaning. If interrogating, deconstructing and reconstructing globalization have become something of an industry among academe and the 'punditariat', its buzzword status has also meant that it can be invoked, with wild imprecision, in virtually any discursive context – including the virtual. (Rowe 2011: 144)

Rowe's observations hold also for the study of the city. Urban studies has been gripped over recent decades by a concern with the global, with terms such as 'global city', 'global city-region' and 'world city', as well as 'globalization', having particular currency. While in some respects it is an outcome of academic fashion, the burgeoning use of these and related concepts nevertheless points to some very real changes in the nature of contemporary urbanization as well as relations between cities and the context of everyday urban life that must be engaged with.

The term 'world city' was first used in 1915 by Patrick Geddes, an influential figure in the development of urban planning in Britain, to describe the then-emerging 'conurbations', such as New York City, which were consuming not just their hinterlands but entire provinces. Peter Hall then reintroduced the term in 1966, using it to define such cities in terms of their multiple roles. World cities were centres of activities, such as government, trade, finance, knowledge, consumption and the arts, and, according to Hall (1977/1966), as the importance of these activities had grown during the twentieth century, so too had the scale and importance of the world city. In 1986 John Friedmann (1986: 69) proposed the existence of a hierarchy of world cities as the ' "basing points" for global capital'. Henri Lefebvre contemplated the issue of the 'global city' and, indeed, the 'globalization of the city' under conditions of complete urbanization, pointing out that the concept of the global city was initially a Maoist one. The task he set himself was to 'extend the traditional concept and image of the city to a global scale: a political centre for the administration, protection, and operation of a vast territory' (Lefebvre 2003a/1970: 169). Urbanization creates new forms of 'global centrality' (Kipfer et al. 2008b: 291) and reshapes the relationship between the centre and the periphery. The city of the future, argues Lefebvre (2003b: 208), 'will inevitably be polycentric, a multiplicity of centres, diversified but conserving a centre. There is no urbanity without a centre.'

It is generally agreed that in the 1970s and 1980s there was an important move 'from an international to a global economy' (Amin and Thrift 1992: 574), and with this shift came the advent of the self-reliant 'global' city. In this respect, Saskia Sassen's (1991) characterization of global cities as the 'command centres' of the global economy and the associated empirical focus on transnational networks of business and finance have been influential in setting the research agenda. Cities such as London, New York and Tokyo, which emerged as the dominant spatial pivots of complex international urban networks of finance, communication and information flows, are frequently regarded as having global city status. Increasingly, in political and economic terms it is global cities rather than nation states that have international hegemony.

> The spatial dispersion of production, including its internationalization, has contributed to the growth of centralized service nodes for the management and regulation of the new space economy. . . . To a considerable extent, the weight of economic activity over the last fifteen years has shifted from production places such as Detroit and Manchester, to centers of finance and highly specialized services. (Sassen 1991: 330–1)

So while 'world cities' are thought to be those that connect local (in its broadest and narrowest senses, including the national and the regional) economies into a world economy, global cities are the locations where the organization of the global economy occurs. Where defining a world city depends on categorization, global cities are regarded as those that are made through the localization of global processes (Robinson 2006: 97).

The positioning or classification of certain cities as world or global cities is both tenuous and arbitrary, but governments and local interest groups nevertheless often put a great deal of effort into obtaining, retaining and asserting such status. For example, in the early 1990s, the London Planning Advisory Committee commissioned a consultancy group to conduct a study to identify what London needed to do to preserve its economic and financial status as a 'world city'. A paper reporting on this study claimed that only London, Tokyo, New York and Paris could 'legitimately' claim to be world cities, while other influential cities, including Milan, Frankfurt, Berlin and Hong Kong, were in the process of pursuing this elite position (Brown 1991: 140). Since the 1990s the concern about world (or even 'world class') city status has itself become a global one, with cities constantly measuring their status and level of global connectedness against other cities and across a range of indicators. The Globalization and World Cities Research Network based at Loughborough University in the United Kingdom has developed an influential classificatory system that ranks cities in groups under a series of labels, including Alpha++, Alpha+, Beta+, Beta, Gamma+, and so on. These rankings are based upon the networks of 175 advanced producer service firms in 525 cities (http://www.lboro.ac.uk/gawc/projects/projec71. html, accessed May 2012). According to these criteria, two cities (London and New York) receive the highest Alpha++ rating, with eight (Beijing, Shanghai, Singapore, Tokyo, Sydney, Milan, Hong Kong and Paris) being ranked as Alpha+.

Similarly, the Institute for Urban Strategies at the Mori Memorial Foundation in Japan has developed its 'Global Power City Index' that supposedly 'evaluates and ranks the major cities of the world according to their comprehensive power to attract creative people and excellent companies from around the world amidst an environment of increasingly strong urban competition worldwide' (Institute for Urban Strategies 2010: 1). The top four cities, according to this index, are New York, London, Paris and Tokyo (in rank order). Likewise, New York, London and Paris occupied the top three positions on the 2010 Knight Frank Global Cities Survey, but a marked shift in the urban geography of global economic power is observed: 'The biggest movements, unsurprisingly, came in our Economic Activity category. The ongoing West-to-East shift in economic might is highlighted by the fact that eight of the 13 jumps in this area were by Asian cities, led by

Shanghai and Kuala Lumpur' (Bailey 2011: np). In looking ahead a decade, this survey predicts that New York and London will continue to occupy the top two spots on the list but Paris will drop to ninth and the 'gap' between the top two cities and the rest will close considerably. And where the 2010 survey has two Asian cities (Tokyo and Beijing) in the top ten, there are six in the 2020 forecast (Tokyo, Beijing, Shanghai, Mumbai, Hong Kong and Singapore).

In a vein that is not dissimilar, there are many commentators who accept that world cities, as the commercial and financial hubs of international activities, such as commodity exchange, insurance and taxation, can be ranked on a continuum or, more accurately, continua. Claims of the existence of urban hierarchies, however, raise a host of unresolved questions, including: what are the elements for defining the ideal-typical world city; and if a continuum can be delineated, on what basis are the cities to be ranked, and what is the legitimacy of the indicators? It continues to be the case that '[p]erception is . . . central to the World City debate' (Brown 1991: 141).

What these indices measure or what purpose they serve beyond place marketing and promotion is something of an open question – for instance, under the heading 'Global Sydney', Sydney City Council boasts on its website the city's rankings on a number of league tables (http://www.cityofsyd-ney.nsw.gov.au/AboutSydney/CityResearch/GlobalSydney. asp, accessed May 2012), and it is very much the case that being or becoming 'world class' according to such indicators is a perennial concern for many postcolonial cities. One of the foundational contributors to the study of globalization and global cities, Anthony King, observed in the early 1990s that '[t]he term "world city" has been around for some time, yet the meanings it signifies have considerably changed' (King 1993: 84; see also King 1990a). He went on to suggest that the most significant shift or blurring of meaning occurred at the beginning of the 1980s, during which time the classifica-tory label 'world city' came to be more than simply a reference to those urban centres that occupied premier positions within the global political economy. Within the nexus of cities around the world, the criteria for assessing the situation occupied by any one city at any particular time now extends beyond the economic and financial to encompass lifestyle, 'liveability' and the cultural/creative (see Chapter 3). Both the possibility and composition of global networks of cities and the globalization of perceptions of the urban as a cultural form are relevant in this context, as are discourses associated with creative cities and global competitions for status, investment and development that have emerged over the last three decades (see Chapters 3 and 7).

The concept of globalization and associated ideas about global cities and world networks of cities are thus complex. Indeed, globalization can be taken to refer to processes which variously create homogeneity, heterogeneity and hybridity. Early claims to the emergence of a global culture, for instance, were made on the assumption that local cultures and diversity would be destroyed by the penetration of dominant 'systems of meaning, action and symbolic forms' (King 1990b: 398), which are usually conceptualized as being American. Although it is clearly the case that the global expansion of American culture and its permeation of other cultural landscapes is an empirical reality, the result of this infiltration has rarely been the demolition of local cultural practices and vitality. Rather, as discussed further below, the more likely scenario is that colonizing practices, values and artefacts may themselves be transformed or subverted in some way as a result of coming into contact with those cultures supposedly being colonized. That said, the colonized culture will often be altered in some way as a result of contact, but the local 'response to globalization' (King 1990b: 398) is more likely to be hybridity and an increase in the production of difference rather than homogeneity. It is unsustainable, therefore, to speak of an all-encompassing 'global culture'.

Importantly, King (1993: 85) points to 'the ideological work which architecture, space and the built environment in general perform in representing the interests of capital on a global scale . . . or the way the changing ethnic, racial or religious composition of cities affects their cultural politics and cultural production with potentially significant local, national and global effects, not least on their economic role'. King's intention is to highlight the intersection of local values and global processes in urban landscapes and its implications. Included in his discussion is a consideration of the local built effects of the global political economy and of international cultural pro-

6.1   Oriental Pearl Tower, Shanghai, China.

duction, including transcontinental multimedia urban events such as the Olympic Games and the FIFA World Cup.

Representations of built space, as aspects of the globalization of both material and symbolic cultural production, also inform popular conceptions not only of which cities should be classified as world or 'world class' cities, but also of what such a city should look like. For instance, landmark towers in central business districts are often constructed to represent a city's attainment of 'world' city status. The tower is perceived to have a legitimacy that is drawn from the existence of similar structures in other major urban centres, a point which is further underlined by the establishment in 1989 of the World Federation of Great Towers (WFGT), an organization which boasts thirty-one 'member towers', including Sydney Tower, the Eiffel Tower in Paris, the Oriental Pearl Tower in Shanghai and, intriguingly, the Empire State Building in New York City (http://www.great-towers.com/#/en/towersa, accessed May 2012). As the WFGT website puts it, '[M]ost of [these] extraordinary buildings have come to symbolize the host cities . . . .' The use of the term 'host city' is particularly interesting in this context as it implicitly references that other marker of 'world' or 'world class' city status and high-profile exercise in city marketing – hosting a global mega-event. The word 'host' not only links to such events, but it also talks to themes of welcome and transience, as if the tower could be picked up and moved to another 'host city' at any given time or the host city could in fact withdraw its hospitality. It is noteworthy, of course, that perhaps the most iconic of urban towers – the Eiffel Tower – was in fact built as a temporary structure for the 1889 World's Fair.

The landmark urban tower is very much an example of the globalization of a particular symbolically significant form of built space. However, as each tower is part of the landscape of its location and not of anywhere else, it remains unique to its place and time, and although the city as a place and as an image may well be reshaped in some way by the construction of the tower, the meanings that are denoted by it are not static and cannot necessarily be transposed from one place to another. They are constantly being defined and redefined through use and over time. They speak simultaneously to the global and the local. To be a symbol of a city is to symbolize uniqueness and local difference as well as to mark a connection with the global. Every city remains a discrete entity that is connected to, but differs from, the other cities of the world and their built landmarks.

*being both global & local.*

Globally circulating ideas, expectations about and impressions of the built form of (world) cities such as New York, London and Paris are highly influential in defining the symbolic parameters of what is meant by the term 'urban'. The semiotic hegemony of such cities informs many of the dominant urban development discourses that have gained currency in cities both within and without the multiplicity of world networks of cities, including the aforementioned landmark tower, skyscrapers, waterfront festival marketplace developments and the now-ubiquitous sightseeing Ferris wheel. Equally, the negative positioning of the urban 'other', such as the stigmatized industrial city or the megacities of the developing South, also occurs within these symbolic limits. As I have discussed elsewhere, however, it is unlikely that the impressions and stereotypes, both positive and negative, that are held by the majority of people regarding how cities 'global' or otherwise might look have been constructed through personal

6.2   Waterfront redevelopment with convention centre and artificial beach in the northern Australian city of Darwin.

contact with, or experience of, each city (Stevenson 1999). Rather, central to the global imagining of built form are international circuits of information and communication, most significantly the production and consumption of film and media imagery and the Internet. Representations of urban landscapes are packaged in the media in a variety of ways and then presented to media consumers around the globe. The travel and tourism media also play important roles in globalizing selected representation of urban space (Wearing et al. 2010).

Rather than there being a single hierarchy of global or world cities, there are, therefore, numerous intersecting global networks and circuits that simultaneously link and separate all cities. Even the so-called 'global economy' is a complex of micro, macro, formal and informal linkages and flows between urban centres. Within these circuits, cities occupy differing positions *vis-à-vis* other cities, nation states and networks of cities on a range of indicators and in a variety of instances.

*[handwritten margin notes: marketing of the city a neoliberal ideal. moulding selected space. construction image of city.]*

These positions may be oppositional or reinforcing, material or symbolic, which is not to deny the significant, often determining, effects that the premier global circuits of political and economic activity have at national, regional and local levels. What it highlights, however, is that it is really not possible to understand any city, its culture or economy without considering its location (aspirational and material) within, outside and in relation to worldwide circuits and flows that reconfigure everyday life and urban space.

## Metropolitan modernity and the 'residual' city

In attempting to move beyond urban hierarchies and the divisions that are constructed/assumed by labels such as 'world', 'global', 'developed' and 'developing' city, geographer Jennifer Robinson (2002, 2006) adopts a term first coined by Ash Amin and Stephen Graham (1997) – 'ordinary cities'. Her point is that urban studies is overly focused on the operation and situation of a limited number of wealthy (Western) cities – those that are enmeshed in the global economy – and excludes, and thus fails to understand, the breadth and diversity of contemporary cities and urban life. Not only that, but this focus is rarely on entire cities but on small highly localized sites within wealthy cities. Rich and prosperous cities contain poor and forgotten areas just as many poor and forgotten cities also have sites of wealth and prosperity. Limited, too, Robinson argues, are the theories and concepts that are available to analyse cities and urbanism because these were developed in the same geographical centres as the cities they privilege. She claims that because dominant urban studies approaches position the wealthy cities of the North as 'originators' – the referents for all things urban – all other (residual) cities are rendered, if not invisible, then 'imitators', even though the majority of urban dwellers live either in the 'othered' cities or the 'othered' parts of major cities, notably in the suburbs, ghettoes and slums.

Robinson seeks to make the complexity and diversity of the 'world of cities' and urban experiences the starting points for a postcolonial approach to urban studies that, she argues, encompasses all cities and parts of cities, including those that are economically (and globally) dominant. In other words, her aim is to broaden the geography of urban knowledge by developing a framework that focuses not on ranked categories but on the diversity of city types, urban populations, local politics and economies, and thus captures the plurality of cities within a single field of analysis. By way of example, she points to the situation of Durban in South Africa, which is a city that sits outside all the established parameters of world-global city status but, as she explains, has a substantial population of three million people and is a major manufacturing city and trading port. A list of similarly positioned cities from around the world can readily be compiled. These cities are not insignificant – a great deal that matters, socially, culturally, economically and emotionally takes place within them and they play important roles both within and beyond the nation state. And yet they are routinely underestimated, devalued or ignored.

Given the hegemony of Western knowledge, the unevenness of cities and urban development and the privileged place of the economy in contemporary society, Robinson's aim is an ambitious and probably unachievable one. But the 'West and the rest' dichotomy is unsustainable, particularly if one accepts that cities and the world of cities are made at the interface of a confluence of networks and rhythms that are linear, circular and distinctive. It is also important to highlight the limitations of those all-embracing, Western-centred approaches to understanding cities and urban processes that have dominated urban studies from the outset. As discussed in Chapter 1, in seeking to develop theories that can be applied universally, urban scholars have frequently assumed the existence of an identifiable and, often, unified urban object. Robinson also highlights the way in which urban studies, urbanization and the foundations of modernity intersect to produce the 'othering' she describes, to wit the privileging of both urban modernity and the processes of urban development that has led to wealthy global cities being associated positively with the achievements and possibilities of modernity, while poorer, often mega, cities are positioned as the objects of a developmentalist agenda. This second point is one to which I will return in Chapter 7.

Mike Savage and Alan Warde (1993) also explain the extent and consequences of the enmeshment of modernity and the study of the urban, suggesting that, largely influenced by Louis Wirth's essay 'Urbanism as a Way of Life' (1995, orig. 1938), urban sociology for a very long time attributed 'the elements of the experience of modernity to urbanisation'. As a result:

> The distinctive features of mundane experience came to be identified as the hallmarks of urban life. Metropolitan cities were seen as repositories of transitory, fleeting and contingent perceptions and relationships; as the locus of fashion, spectacle and novelty; as sites where new levels of personal anxiety, uncertainty, anonymity and dislocation emerged. These characteristics we now perceive as the traits of modernity. (Savage and Warde 1993: 189)

Similarly, the shape and experience of the urban are attributed to modernity. Savage and Warde (1993) further argue that the conflation continued into the 1970s, even within Marxist urban studies, which regarded the urban experiences of modernity as the outcomes not of urbanization and urban environments, but of the organization of capitalism. As a result, influential sociologists such as Manuel Castells (1972) treated urban modernity and capitalism analytically as being causally connected rather than related but discrete. Savage and Warde (1993) make the additional point that understanding the ways in which these separate-but-linked processes affect the city should be a central concern of the agenda of urban sociology and thus of urban studies. Robinson's (2006) thesis is not dissimilar, although, drawing on empirical research, she seeks to extend the analysis to contemplate the consequences on the ground of fusing modernity and the urban. Positioning the urban as modern by definition implicitly posits the non-urban, non-modern 'other' as primitive and backward. But of course it is more complex than this, and what constitutes the global North and South shifts. As I have argued elsewhere, this othering is also played out in the rural–urban dichotomy, which continues to be influential within urban studies as well as between cities within nations (Stevenson 2003). Wirth (1995), for instance, in considering the parameters of the urban, does so by explicitly contrasting urbanism (unfavourably) with the rural 'other' of tradition, solidarity and community.

It was Georg Simmel, in 1903, who was the first to problematize the idea and culture of the city in the context of modernity (Simmel 1995). Unlike other urban theorists and sociologists of his time, however, his analysis of urbanism was neither grounded in nostalgia for rural life nor was it deeply disdainful of the city. Indeed, as explained in Chapter 5 above, Simmel's was in many ways a celebration of the urban. His concern was to understand 'the specifically modern aspects of contemporary life', and as modernity had in his view found its most evident expression in the emerging cities of the West, the city and urbanism were the almost accidental objects of his attention. Setting Simmel's urban analysis apart from those of others, such as the Chicago School, is his view that the city is more than a place of difference and the routine spatial proximity of strangers – 'the circulation and interaction of bodies' (Frisby 2007: 143); also entrenched in the social structures and everyday circumstances of the modern metropolis are the contradictory but dialectical conditions of freedom and isolation. In other words, the factors that separate city dwellers from each other and create experiences and feelings of loneliness are the very same conditions that make freedom possible: 'If *increasing* social differentiation is a developmental tendency in modernity, for Simmel, then that accentuation of differentiation at a variety of levels is especially evident in metropolitan centres . . .' (Frisby 2007: 152).

Simmel argues that it is the increase in number, spatiality and 'the meaningful content of life' that is intrinsic to the modern urban environment that has enabled individuals to experience a freedom of movement, association and ideas not otherwise possible. In this respect, his celebration of metropolitan modernity is strong: '[T]he citizen of the metropolis is "free" in contrast with the trivialities and prejudices which bind the small town person. The mutual reserve and indifference, and the intellectual conditions of life in large social units are never more sharply appreciated in their significance for the independence of the individual than in the dense crowds of the metropolis . . .' (Simmel 1995: 40). Feminists have also questioned the universality of the freedoms associated with urban modernity and have been keen to point out that women rarely occupy urban space in the ways that men do, and that what may be described as freedom for a man may well be experienced by a woman as constraint (Wolff 1985; also see Chapter 4).

London, Paris and Berlin were at the centre of the emerging 'urban modernity' of the North, but in many respects it was New York City (or at least Manhattan) that emerged as perhaps the quintessential symbol of metropolitan modernity – of progress, achievement and 'man's' ability to triumph over nature. This is a status which New York assumed not simply because of its geographical size and global economic dominance, but also as a result of its landscapes of iconic buildings that served to mark the city as powerful, wealthy and modern (Stevenson 2003: 1–3). In the conceptual shadow of the modern Northern city, however, are regional and 'small' (Bell and Jayne 2006) cities as well as the megacities of the developing South or 'third world' which feature prominently on any list of the world's most populous cities and less often on the lists of the economically or culturally powerful. Cities such as São Paulo, Mumbai and Mexico City are all rendered outside the frames of the modern, cosmopolitan metropolis. Theirs, in part, is an urban status marked by overcrowding, overt poverty, poor housing stock and vast areas of failing or non-existent basic services, such as sewerage and access to clean water. And to invoke another league table, this observation is borne out by the Quality of Life rankings of the 2011 Knight Frank Global Cities Survey, which includes only one Asian city – Tokyo at number seven – in its 'top ten'. At the same time, the cities of the South dominate the list of 'megacities' with populations in excess of ten million people. It is noteworthy also that Savage and Warde's important 1993 book, which focused on 'urban sociology, capitalism and modernity' is concerned with the cities and perspectives of the North.

Robinson (2006: 13) argues that the privileging of modernity by urban studies has positioned (ranked) seemingly non-modern/non-Western cities as lacking in terms of quality of life and services and thus in need of development: 'Where the global-world city approach generalises the successful locales of high-finance and corporate city life, the developmentalist approach tends towards a vision of all poor cities as infrastructurally poor and economically stagnant yet (perversely?)

expanding in size.' The rapid economic growth that is occurring in many 'developing' cities suggests, however, that they are no longer economically stagnant nor will they continue to fall off the maps fashioned by urban hierarchies. These cities are being built and lived at the interface of the circuits and discourses that create both (under)development and prosperity, and an expanding and increasingly affluent middle and professional class occupies the spaces of privilege in the cities of the South as surely as it does in a global metropole. Moreover, many commentators have pointed to the 'third world' living conditions of the urban poor in the cities of the West, where an alarmingly large number of people lack access to health care, housing and other basic services as an outcome in part of neoliberalism.

As urban studies grapples with issues of globalization and its local effects, and the core and the periphery, new ways of understanding cities and their diversity are being explored, including, as discussed above, the abandonment of narrow urban hierarchies and labels and the development of conceptual frames that can deal more effectively with urban complexity and the everyday diversity of cities. It is also necessary to look more closely at conceptualizations of the local.

## Localities in the margins

The growth of the global economy and increasingly globalized forms of media and communication, along with the development of so-called 'global cities' and the international circuits and networks that constitute and link them, has reshaped the geography of the core and the periphery. At its simplest, it is the 'global city and the rest' dichotomy that is at issue here, but also reconfigured are other spatial relationships, including those between nations, the city centre and the suburbs, the metropolis and the region, the rural and the urban, and the global and the local. There have also been assertions from some within urban studies that the increasing importance being attributed to place and the local is occurring in response to the seemingly totalizing discourses, hierarchies and processes of globalization. It is in this context, too, that prominence has been given to questions of difference and the building and marketing of cities and urban spaces that attempt overtly to speak to the local and the idiosyncratic – 'place making' is not simply a global buzzword; it is also deeply embedded in processes of reshaping urban space in ways intended to resonate with local cultures and communities (Stevenson forthcoming).

With respect to the spatial unevenness of investment and the socio-economic conditions that produce extremes of urban wealth and poverty, Sassen (2010b: 286) talks about 'geographies of centrality and marginality' where '[t]he downtowns of cities and business centres receive massive investments in real estate and telecommunications.... At the same time, low-income urban and metropolitan areas are starved of resources, with New York City's ghetto areas in Brooklyn and the many shanty towns in Mexico City two brutal instances.' In other words, where once the global divide was between the cities of the West and those of the 'non-modern, developing' rest, it now cuts through at both the national and international scales. For instance, while many formerly prosperous industrial cities of the West have been rendered 'peripheral', nearby major cities and centres of finance, commerce and culture have increased in wealth and prosperity – 'the condition of being peripheral is installed in different geographic terrains depending on the prevailing economic dynamics' (Sassen 2000: 210). In a slightly different context, Lefebvre once observed that 'wherever a dominated space is generated and mastered by a dominant space – where there is periphery and centre – there is colonization' (quoted in Kipfer and Goonewardena 2007: 37). Colonization, according to this formulation, refers not just to imperialist relations between nations under conditions of neoliberalism, but also to relations within nations between the metropolis and the regional urban other.

Globalization and the shaping of 'global space' at its most extreme conceptualization suggest the obliteration of space, if not by time, then by possibility and transcendence. As Doreen Massey (2008: 81) explains, globalization conjures 'a vision of total unfettered mobility; of free unbounded space'. This is a space without borders or barriers comprised of global flows and circuits. But rather than this 'space of flows' annihilating the 'space of places' (Castells 1991), the global is, in fact, simultaneously a space of places formed at the intersection (location) of the global. In other words, as Massey (2008: 83) also points out, globalization 'is a making of space(s), an active reconfiguration and meeting-up through practices and relations of a multitude of trajectories'. Localities, which, according to Castells (1991: 351), 'can become indispensable elements in the new economic geography', are not just, or even necessarily, cities (global, international or world). Rather, and although cities are important, also constituted through the discourses and circuits of globalization are the towns, suburbs, regions and by-ways which may be on the margins of the global economy but are very much at the centre of the social and cultural formation and experience of everyday life and of nation states. In recognizing the importance of place, Castells (1991: 151) makes the following point:

> At the cultural level, local societies, territorially defined, must preserve their identities, and build upon their historical roots, regardless of their economic and functional dependence upon the space of flows. The symbolic making of places, the preservation of symbols of recognition, the expression of collective memory in actual practices of communication, are fundamental means by which places may continue to exist . . . .

Similarly, for Massey (1991: 275), localities 'are not just about physical buildings, nor even about capital momentarily imprisoned; they are about the intersection of social activities and social relations and, crucially, activities and relations which are necessarily, by definition, dynamic, changing'.

An influential strand of locality-focused research emerged in the United Kingdom during the 1980s that was concerned to examine the effects of deindustrialization and globalization on specific localities, including Liverpool, Lancaster and Birmingham (Bagguley et al. 1990; Cooke 1989; Harloe et al. 1990; Savage et al. 1987). The starting point for this research was the realization that national and international changes to the economy and the nature of industrialism were affecting different regions and localities in different ways (Massey 1991), combined with the belief 'not that . . . localities can be studied in isolation, but that broader processes do not fully explain what happens in particular places' (Pickvance 1990: 1). It was thought that in-depth locality research could provide important insights into the extent and nature of global processes as well as into the place-specific policies and platforms for political action that were developing in response to the local consequences of these processes.

In many ways, locality research highlights the resonance of the view put forward by Lefebvre a decade before this research was under way. Nevertheless, the locality studies were strongly criticized by many within urban studies on a range of methodological and epistemological grounds, and for being overly concerned with contingency and specificity (the micro) at the expense of the structural (the macro). It was argued, for instance, that research focused on local responses to significant economic change was highly conservative and often trivialized the significance and extent of macro processes and class-based inequalities and undermined the potential for fundamental social action and structural change. David Harvey (1987) was a high-profile critic of the localities research because of what he saw as a shift in the focus of Marxist urban studies away from the capitalist mode of production to the processes and practices of consumption. Even so, he acknowledged that some consideration of the local level could be valuable and had the potential to play a role in the 'search for global solutions' (Harvey 1987: 376).

The focus on place and locality, whilst assuming a very specific complexion in recent years in the context of globalization and neoliberalism, is not new within urban studies. As discussed in Chapter 1, the work of the Chicago School throughout much of the twentieth century was concerned with the study of localities, including of the everyday life in these places. Building, in part, on the Chicago School was the community studies tradition, which involved researchers undertaking ethnographic research into all aspects of life in suburbs, towns and neighbourhoods. Influential in shaping these studies of community and urbanism was the work in the late nineteenth century of Ferdinand Tönnies (1957/1887), who sought to explain the social change (including a rupturing of traditional social ties) that was occurring as a result of rapid urbanization and industrialization. To this end, he developed an evolutionary model that categorized relationships within settlement types in terms of *Gemeinschaft* (community) and *Gesellschaft* (society). According to Tönnies, *Gemeinschaft* relationships are those which are intimate, enduring and exist between people with kinship, friendship and neighbourhood ties. These are typical of the relationships he claimed were found in small towns and villages, in contrast to *Gesellschaft* relationships, which, being impersonal and often contractual, were in his view characteristic of the urban condition.

In 1962, Herbert Gans replaced the concepts *Gemeinschaft* and *Gesellschaft* with a tripartite formulation that categorized relationships as being primary, secondary and quasi-primary. Primary relationships, he argued, typically exist between family members and close friends; secondary relationships are those casual associations that people have with storekeepers and bureaucrats; and 'quasi-primary' relationships are those that are more intimate than secondary but more guarded than primary relationships. What Gans had in mind was the sociality that, he suggested, develops between neighbours in new suburban areas. These suburban estates, he said, were often the 'highly visible showcase for the (quasi-primary) way of life of young, upper-working-class and lower-middle-class people' (Gans 1962: 632).

For Gans, neighbourhood-based quasi-primary relationships were the outcome of homogeneity in the life-cycle stage and the social class of residents. Gans (1962: 635, 644) went on to suggest that people often chose to live in the suburbs because they were seeking the quasi-primary neighbourhood relationships that they believed were characteristic of such areas. Over time, however, and with residential change, neighbourhood-based quasi-primary relationships often broke down and were replaced by those that were secondary. He argued that this would be the fate of the predominantly working-class inner-city neighbourhoods, which at the time he was writing were in a state of 'transition'. What many 'transitioned' into, of course, were the gentrified neighbourhoods of the new (creative) middle class (see Chapter 2). In a postscript to a 1995 reprinting of his 1962 essay, Gans (1995: 188) acknowledges the diversity of the suburbs, saying that they had become home to people of 'all ages and household types' and not just to young families.

Community studies – and, in particular, the ethnographic methodology that is associated with this form of research – remains unrivalled in its ability to expose the texture and detail of everyday urban life. And although the community studies tradition stands rightly accused of being uncritical and atheoretical (Savage and Warde, 1993: 105), there are studies that have been undertaken by researchers concerned to explore structural issues, such as stratification, family and gender relations within a particular locality. As did the locality studies discussed above, these community studies have provided rich insights into the relationship between the micro sites of everyday life and the macro structures and power relations which constrain experience (Bryson and Thompson 1972; Oxley 1973).

Community and locality studies can, therefore, in different ways reveal the 'everyday meanings to which people do attach importance and which to them appear unproblematic' (Harvey 1992: 598). More recently, within sociology and geography there has been something of a revival of interest in the local as part of a broader research agenda examining identity, place and belonging. In addition, and largely following the work of Zygmunt Bauman (2011a/2001, 2011b/2000), is research that examines what community might mean under conditions of globalization. Bauman (2011a/2001: 15) warns, however, that the idea of identity has become something of a 'surrogate for community' in that it privileges the individual over commonality, autonomy over interdependence. As a society of individuals, Bauman suggests that people increasingly fear (and actively seek to avoid) difference, diversity and the 'other'. The challenge of reconceptualizing and reasserting the importance of community is first to identify what constitutes community in a 'world of individuals'. Here his starting point is an ethic of care and mutual responsibility (Bauman 2011a/2001: 149–50). The scope of the challenge Bauman presents should not be underestimated, but it is clear that the city and urban life must be part of any such reconceptualization. In particular, it will be necessary to rethink the relationship between the global and the local as it is usually understood, including uncoupling community from the rural, the small and the face-to-face.

# Conclusion

The processes of globalization have reshaped economies, cities, societies and cultures. Globalization is also instrumental in creating the conditions for the establishment of hierarchies and league tables which measure and rank cities according to an ever-expanding range of indicators, including residential quality of life, status as a financial centre and the significance of the networks of which a city is part. Cities are now locked into a raft of inter-urban competitions to attract capital, tourists and the 'creative class' (to name but three) and to improve their global position. To some extent, such status is rather arbitrary but it is, nevertheless, the case that a small number of cities are routinely named at the top of such rankings. The aim of this chapter was to examine some of these issues and the different ways in which cities are understood in relation to the global. To this end, it considered the so-called 'global' and 'world' cities theses, pointing out that where the label 'global city' is generally applied to those cities that play pivotal roles in the organization of the global economy, world cities are those that link the local into the world.

The chapter argued that globalization is not only a set of processes and intersections that have shape and consequences, but it is also based implicitly on inclusion and exclusion, a central core and marginalized periphery. Entire cities and parts of cities routinely fall outside what is conceptualized as the global. There are a number of reasons for this, including the diversity and complexity of cities that can simultaneously house the spaces of prosperity and those of poverty and disadvantage. The chapter went on to suggest that the focus on the global has prompted many to wonder about the consequences for those localities that although outside its networks and discourses are increasingly defined in terms of, and with reference to, the global. Neoliberalism and globalization combined were central to the conditions which led to the withdrawal of manufacturing industries from many cities in the nations of the North. But there are also other factors at play, including a fusing of the global-urban with modernity and the North, and the 'othering' of the non-modern, non-Western, non-Northern. It may be, as some have suggested, that it is time to move beyond narrow conceptualizations of the city in the context of globalization and engage instead with the complexity of cities and urban life. But the trends seem to be otherwise, and in recent years there has been a proliferation of city visions, plans and branding strategies which are designed to help cities reposition their economies and images *vis-à-vis* the global. A consideration of these influential conceptualizations of the city is the concern of the next chapter.

# 7
# Imagined City

## Visions and Brands

> It would be convenient . . . to regard the city, not as a mere congeries of persons and social arrangements, but as an institution.
>
> Park 1915: 577

## Introduction

In the quest for a position on one or more global hierarchies of cities, perhaps to gain status as a 'world class city' or to attract capital investment, ~~an increasing number of cities have become preoccupied with adopting globally circulating reimaging and redevelopment strategies and visions.~~ The ~~result has been an upsurge of branding, theming and place marketing.~~ Terms such as 'brandscape' have entered the lexicon of planners, and many cities seek to gain some advantage in this global competition of cities by engaging a celebrity 'starchitect' to design a signature building as an iconic marker of the city. While so-called 'second', often deindustrializing, cities have embraced these approaches with particular enthusiasm, established 'world' and 'global' cities have also been keen to adopt a range of city imaging and reprofiling strategies, including landmark building projects and hosting mega-events such as the Olympic Games. ~~Branding, visioning and reimaging strategies and processes reveal~~

a great deal about the relationship between capitalism and the urban as well as about the way in which neoliberalism intersects with governance to reshape environments. Also revealed is the potency of the networks and exchanges that increasingly shape cities. Consultants circulate the globe advising local governments and business interests as to which of the many 'off-the-shelf' reimaging strategies they should adopt. So while city visioning is supposedly about the local, it has been a key factor limiting the role of the local in decision-making.

In exploring these issues, this chapter traces the rise of city branding and 'brandscaping' in the context of an increasingly entrepreneurial approach to city building and governance. Flagship and brand stores as well as signature architecture are each discussed in this context. The chapter goes on to consider the rise of the contemporary mega-mall as a leisure, entertainment and shopping space that is itself an event destination. Although these spaces are spectacular in their size, content and appearance, they are at the same time predictable, standardized, homogenized and sanitized. There is no place within these landscapes for either serendipity or the non-consumer. Through the operation of transnational bodies such as the World Bank and UNESCO, cities in poor countries have also increasingly become ensnared in international networks, processes and the agendas of city visioning, and the final section of the chapter considers the use of formal city development strategies as illustrative of this process. While these strategies are intended to provide a framework for crafting a city vision that is grounded in the priorities and diversity of local communities, this aim presents a number of challenges. The chapter concludes with a brief consideration of the vexed issue of consultation and participation in city planning and imaging.

## Themes in the landscape

Over the last thirty years, the belief that architecture, urban planning and design can play central roles in shaping the identity or image of entire cities and/or districts within cities has gained considerable currency with local authorities, residents and commercial interests. As a result, and often in response to the spatial consequences of changed economic circumstances and the quest for 'global' status, there has been a proliferation of city-focused reimaging strategies that, in attempting to mark (and market) cities as being different, are designed to attract tourists, business investment and residents (the 'creative class'). As discussed in previous chapters, the arts and cultural industries frequently occupy prominent positions in such strategies; so too do special events, knowledge and innovation, and often also involved is the wholesale redevelopment of ruined or abandoned city precincts. In addition, and as also outlined in previous chapters, the gentrification of inner-city neighbourhoods is routinely now positioned as a key aim of city reimaging and redevelopment schemes, and so it is common for the provision of housing for middle- and high-income earners to be prioritized along with the building of upmarket leisure and cultural facilities. What is being sold in city reimaging and promotion strategies is not simply the physical (often redeveloped) spaces of the city, but also its symbolic spaces, including how the city feels, what it means and what it looks like (Ashworth and Voogd 1990; Kearns and Philo 1993). The term 'urban tourism' is often used with reference to a range of reimaging and promotional measures associated with the provision of purpose-built leisure, cultural and recreational facilities and resources, many of which are explicitly promoted to attract visitors (Wearing et al. 2010).

Another important element of place marketing is the practice of city branding, which has developed as a complex of advertising, visions and narratives, as well as catchy (official and unofficial) city slogans and mottos (Kavaratzis 2004), with 'Glasgow's Miles Better', 'I ♥ New York', 'I Amsterdam' and 'City of Angels' being four city slogans, developed for very different purposes, that come readily to mind. A brand is both a statement and a promise. It is intended to be a sign or marker of a place and the experience of being in that place – to move reimaging beyond the functional to the imaginative and representational. A city's brand(s) can be crafted to speak variously and sometimes simultaneously to a city's past, present and future and is usually designed to highlight – summarize – those features and qualities of the city that supposedly are unique or special. Not surprisingly, developing a resonant city brand can be a fraught and often highly contentious process. Stephanie Hemelryk Donald and John G. Gammack (2007: 45) argue, for instance,

> that branding has entered . . . debates in an attempt to capture and shape the city as a product and knowable entity for residents and visitors. While brand creation and brand maintenance for goods and services have become an immensely sophisticated industry and set of practices, 'destination' and – especially – 'city' branding pose a yet more complex layer of challenge, identifications, and contradictions.

City branding is a process of inclusion and exclusion that privileges and highlights some aspects and ways of understanding a city while marginalizing others. Not only do some interests stand to benefit from city imaging and place marketing at the expense of other interests, but various interests have different, often incompatible, perceptions of 'their city'. The brand as well as the process and rationale for determining it are thus the outcomes of relative power. As discussed below, even branding processes that are seemingly designed to engage

7.1  'I Amsterdam' sign, the Netherlands.

with a broad range of local interests inevitably prioritize
limited agendas and ways of seeing (Stevenson 1999).

The emergence of city branding can be traced to the rise of
neoliberalism and specifically to what has been called the
'entrepreneurial city' (Hall and Hubbard 1998; see also
Chapter 2), whereby cities are increasingly run as businesses
and the practices of business are applied to the processes of
urban governance. It was the entrepreneurial approach to city
governance that led to the techniques and methods of product
marketing being applied to the promotion of the city. Indeed,
Phil Hubbard and Tim Hall (1998: 8) acknowledge that 'the
manipulation of city images, cultures and experiences has
become probably the most important part of the political
armoury of urban governors and their coalition partners in the
entrepreneurial era'. They go on to outline the contours of the
generic model of entrepreneurial governance as being focused
on city marketing, urban redevelopment, staging mega-events,
the use of the arts and cultural industries and of public–private
partnerships (involving governments entering into an alliance
with the private sector) as ways of attracting external investment and funding the infrastructure that (it is believed) will
foster local economic development. With a somewhat different
emphasis, urban entrepreneurialism is also examined by David
Harvey, who foregrounds, in particular, the importance of
(global) inter-urban competition for capital investment in city
redevelopment and reimaging, and the reshaping of urban
governance. For Harvey (1989b: 12), the move from 'managerialism to entrepreneurialism' is implicated in the shift from
'locationally rather rigid Fordist production systems backed
by Keynesian state welfarism to a much more geographically
open and market based form of flexible accumulation'. In
addition, according to Harvey (1989b: 7), the public–private
partnerships that are at the centre of the processes of entrepreneurial governance are 'speculative in execution and design'
and involve, if not the profits of the private sector being under-
written by the public sector which carries the risk, then the
local state overtly facilitating the interests of capitalism.

John R. Logan and Harvey Molotch (2007), building on
Molotch's classic 1976 article 'The City as a Growth Machine',
also probe the nexus between city building, the interests of
coalitions of business interests, including property developers

and real estate agents, and the political class. They summarize
how in the United States the 'growth machine'

> use[s] city hall, the state capital and – insofar as they can get
> into them – the halls of Congress to generate growth for their
> metropolis as a whole and for the section of it in particular . . . .
> [T]he city *becomes* a growth machine, and its custodians are
> the people who grease its wheels, refurbish its parts, and tweak
> its direction as the need arises . . . . [F]or one group, the city *is*
> their business. (Logan and Molotch 2007: x)

Logan and Molotch set out to reveal the intricate processes of,
and the role of key urban actors in, what Henri Lefebvre terms
the production of space. Importantly, in probing the dynamics
of the production of space, a central concept in their formulation is culture because, they argue, the capitalist market is the
product of culture at the same time as it works through the
'human interests of wealth, power and affection' (Logan and
Molotch 2007: 9).

"brand-
scape"

The notion of city branding points to the manipulation of
place image and city marketing strategies and the power of
urban interests, as well as increasingly to the presence of
brands in the landscape. The 'brandscape' – a term coined to
refer to this proliferation of city brands and brand-related
products (Sherry 1987) – is a highly interactive, three-
dimensional space that simultaneously advertises products and
marks/creates cityspace. When thinking of brandscapes, Times
Square in New York City is perhaps the place that comes most
readily to mind. Times Square is awash with neon signs, bill-
boards and video screens which bombard the senses with
advertisements for a raft of products and brands, such as
Samsung, Coca-Cola, Disney and HSBC, as well as promo-
tions for movie screenings, sporting events and the latest
Broadway shows. It also advertises nations – for instance, in
January 2011, to coincide with the visit of its President, Hu
Jintao, to the United States, China arranged the high-repetition
screening of a sixty-second promotional video on a series of
billboard-size screens on Times Square. Described as a 'public
diplomacy campaign', the videos ran 300 times a day for about
a month (Barron 2011). Street advertising is more important
in marking and making this particular urban space than the
buildings, roads and footpaths, which are rendered almost to

the status of backdrop. Times Square is also an instantly re-cognizable marker of New York City and the focal point for many of the city's public celebrations, including, most notably, the New Year's Eve countdown, when the now-famous 'New Year's Eve Ball' descends the flagpole at One Times Square.

Anna Klingmann (2010) argues that brandscapes are more than the proliferation of advertising signs in the landscape and that architecture is not simply a backdrop to the branding process. Signature buildings, for instance, are important ele-ments of the branded landscape and frequently are highly visible markers of corporate power. As discussed in Chapter 6, architecture can also be used to convey what a city is and what it wants to be. Klingmann explains that with the emer-gence of the 'experience economy' in the 1990s, architecture moved away from being simply functional to being an expres-sion of the identity of the building owner and, in turn, fre-quently a marker more broadly – as icon – of the city. Architecture, she suggests, spatializes the brand. Klingmann points to the importance of themed 'brand' and 'flagship brand' stores to this restructuring of the brand. She suggests that the emergence of flagship stores such as Niketown and Prada Epicenter took the idea of the brand and translated it quite literally into an all-enveloping experience. People go to a flagship store for the experience as much as for the products on offer – one only has to spend a little time in any Apple flagship store to see this phenomenon in action. Similarly, going to Starbucks is not just about buying a cup of coffee but also about consuming the brand. The geography of the brand-scape thus moves beyond function to being highly immersive. Brands mould ideas and experience; they can confer prestige or a particular type of status on both the consumer and the space.

So as a central element of the branded landscape, the flag-ship store is not the neutral backdrop to, or support for, bill-boards and signs; rather, it is a sign in itself. While flagship stores can be explicitly branded with company logos or names, in many cases, such as the Prada Epicenters example, the branded environment that is the flagship store does not actu-ally involve the overt use of signs at all but relies instead on often subtle architectural and style codes. Such stores speak to the elegance, exclusivity and sophistication of both the product and the consumer. The central notion here is that of the insider – those consumers with the cultural capital required to 'read' the embedded codes and the economic capital to be able to shop there. According to Robert V. Kozinets et al. (2002: 17), flagship brand stores have three distinguishing characteristics: 'First, they carry a single (usually established) brand of product. Second, that brand's manufacturer owns them. Finally, they are operated – at least in part – with the intention of building or reinforcing the image of the brand rather than operating to sell product at a profit.' They go on to suggest that with the flagship store, manufacturers are entering not only the retailing industry but also the 'entertainment business'.

The contemporary brandscape, suggests Klingmann (2010), also includes the hotel industry. For instance, the W hotel chain uses architecture and design as part of a strategy to mark each of its hotels as unique – different in form and image from the generic 'international' hotel. As explained on the hotel website: 'W Hotels is an innovative, contemporary, design-led lifestyle brand and the hotel category buster . . . . Inspiring, iconic, innovative and influential, W Hotels provides the ultimate in insider access to a world of "Wow." Each hotel offers a unique mix of innovative design and passions around fashion, music and entertainment' (http://www.starwoodhotels.com/whotels/about/index.html, accessed April 2011, quote no longer online).

The performance of brandscaping combined with the global competitions that now exist between cities has been influential also in prompting the emergence of the celebrity architect. People such as Frank Gehry, Tadao Ando, Richard Meier, Renzo Piano and Zaha Hadid, among others, are serially engaged to produce signature, landmark buildings in cities around the world. Significant here is what has come to be known as the 'Bilbao effect' or 'Bilbao factor', which refers to the international trend that followed the opening in 1997 of the Frank Gehry-designed Guggenheim Museum in the provincial Spanish city of Bilbao. Built on a rundown former industrial site, the museum brought considerable prestige and economic benefits to the city, including an increase in tourism. It also led to the routine inclusion of a celebrity architect commission in many city branding and reimaging strategies, the rationale being that while very few cities will be selected as locations for a Guggenheim Museum, any city can have a signature building that has been designed by a 'starchitect' (McNeill 2008). The cities of the Middle East, and Dubai in particular, stand out as emblematic of this trend, but there are others. For instance, since becoming the capital of the post-Soviet nation of Kazakhstan in 1997, Astana has been the object of a highly ambitious programme of city building and branding which includes the construction of a number of landmark buildings designed by leading architects, notably Norman Foster.

Celebrity architects bring to the brandscape recognizable built icons. This is not in itself a new phenomenon, of course – the landmark Guggenheim Museum in New York City, for instance, which opened in 1959, was designed by renowned architect Frank Lloyd Wright – but the context in which signature architecture and the 'starchitect' have emerged is very different. Architecture in the age of celebrity and the entrepreneurial city is intended to put a signature to the brand as part of broader global processes of city imaging and inter-urban competition. With brandscaping, however, also comes the risk of seriality and predictability. Twenty-first-century signature buildings may eventually homogenize cityscapes, just as Starbucks or McDonald's and other brand and flagship stores have done. There is also a risk that their replication will adversely affect local business, economies and cultures. Many have noted, for instance, the sameness of British high streets, which have come to be dominated by chain brand stores. Also important in this context is the staging of mega-events (in particular the Olympic Games) involving large-scale urban redevelopment and the building of themed landscapes, such as waterfront developments, shopping malls and landmark buildings intended to be central aspects of the urban legacy of the event.

## Immobilizing the spectacle

Post-Second World War urbanization, and particularly the mass suburban development that was one of its distinguishing features (see Chapter 3), simultaneously reshaped the demographic maps of cities in the West and the nature and spatiality of leisure and retailing. The movement of a large proportion of the population away from the inner city to the urban fringes combined with increased levels of household affluence was also a pivotal factor in the growth of suburban shopping malls. At the same time, many traditional strip shopping centres became increasingly dominated by brand stores and large retailing chains, which, according to Thad Williamson et al. (2005: 317), 'thrived' in these environments, with the US mega-chain store Wal-Mart (one of the largest retailers and public corporations in the world) being at the forefront of this form of development. To illustrate the scale of the shift in the nature of retailing, Williamson et al. go on to point out that in 1950 there were only 100 shopping centres in the United States, but by 1992 (the peak of the shopping mall building boom) there were approaching 40,000 and there are now no doubt many more. Not only have shopping malls proliferated globally since the 1950s, but they have also become bigger and more complex. Indeed, they effectively blur the line between entertainment and consumption (Amin and Thrift 2008: 124). The contemporary shopping mall can simultaneously be shopping centre, theme park and entertainment space – an event destination in its own right. For instance, the largest enclosed shopping mall in the world, the Dubai Mall, houses among other attractions an ice-skating rink, an aquarium, an indoor theme park, a twenty-two-screen cinema and a zoo, as well as numerous food outlets and over 1,000 speciality shops and department stores (http://www.thedubaimall.com/en, accessed May 2012). As is the case with all such shopping malls, the Dubai Mall is a total environment; it is inward-looking and utilizes architecture, design, performance and entertainment to attract people to the mall and then to keep them there and consuming for as long as possible. Dave Hill's description of the West Edmonton Mall in Canada is apt:

> The pursuit of aimless leisure here approaches the surreal. . . . [It] is not so much a shopping city as a fully integrated consumer fantasy that succeeds in being mindlessly mellifluous, utterly ridiculous and absolutely out of this world. . . . The pleasure is in being part of a quietly lunatic alternative universe where the thin line that divides shopping from enter-

7.2 Dubai Mall aquarium.

tainment . . . [is] almost universally erased. (cited in Bauman 1994: 150–1)

Ash Amin and Nigel Thrift (2008: 125) suggest that there are four characteristics of contemporary themed commercial centres, including mega-shopping malls. First, these spaces are designed to facilitate various forms of interaction between consumers and other consumers, and consumers and the spaces of the centre. The environment is also highly theatrical with, second, 'carefully scripted performances' and, third, the use of a variety of media to stimulate the imagination of visitors and create a multidimensional sensory experience. And finally, these spaces and their uses are closely monitored and adjustments are made as necessary to the space, its programming and presentation in response to the reactions of 'audiences'. Themed commercial centres are first and foremost sites of consumption, and through the utilization of seductive spatial, sensory and marketing tactics people are encouraged to consume. Surveillance also plays an important role in the landscape of the shopping mall both to ensure the security of the consumer and to protect private property and the interests of retailers (see Chapter 4). But the ethos that links consumption and experience has broken free of the shopping mall and there are now a range of spaces designed according to similar principles: notable here is the serial transformation of waterfront sites into themed places for leisure and retail activities (Stevenson 2003), while airports too are frequently sites for event shopping (Wearing et al. 2010).

The trend towards theming and building standardized forms of urban space has been examined by many within urban studies, with Mark Gottdiener's *The Theming of America* (1997) and Michael Sorkin's anthology *Variations on a Theme Park* (1992) being two important works. Similarly, the influence of theming and the ethos of branding, not only on cities, but also on society more broadly, has been much discussed in the sociology literature. George Ritzer (1993), for instance, coined the evocative term 'McDonaldization' to describe 'the process by which the principles of the McDonald's fast-food restaurant chain were infiltrating more and more aspects of society' (Ritzer 1993: 3). According to this thesis, McDonaldization is the process by which the world is 'growing increasingly efficient, calculable, predictable and dominated by controlling non-human technologies' (Ritzer and Liska 1997: 97). These dimensions of standardization and homogenization are thriving under conditions of globalization, materialism and neoliberalism. McDonaldization is a ('contemporary') reworking of Max Weber's rationalization thesis and, as is the case with Weber's conceptualization, Ritzer also presents a rather pessimistic and 'dystopian' assessment of society. Following Weber, he argues that rationality, and thus McDonaldization, is ultimately irrational because 'rational systems are unreasonable systems ... that ... deny the basic humanity, the human reason, of the people who work within or are served by them' (Ritzer 1993: 154). Ritzer and others have examined through the lens of McDonaldization many (serial) aspects of contemporary (rational) city building, including suburban tract housing, shopping malls, hotels and fast-food outlets, to name but four.

Drawing on the notion of McDonaldization, Alan Bryman (1999) proposed the related concept of Disneyization, not as a process of increasing rationalization, but to describe the proliferation of the philosophy exemplified by Disney theme parks. Where Ritzer's point of departure is rationality and modernity, Bryman's is consumption and the idea of the consumer society. Working from this conceptualization of society, he aims to 'identify large-scale changes that are discernible in economy and culture that can be found in, and are symbolized by, the Disney parks' (Bryman 1999: 29). To this end, Bryman suggests four features which have flourished beyond the parks: the theming of more and more aspects of everyday life; the dedifferentiation of consumption exemplified by the merging of shopping and the theme park; the mass merchandising of products, such as Disney characters and overtly branded clothing, that are manufactured under licence and sold in outlets around the world; and, finally, the expectation that workers, in particular those in the service industries, will express a contrived range of emotions, such as friendliness, in their dealings with customers – what Bryman terms 'emotional labour'. John Hannigan (1998) brings together themes such as McDonaldization and Disneyization to explain the 'fantasy city' that emerged in the late twentieth century. This city was formed by the merging of several trends: the increased rationalization of production following the principles of McDonaldization – efficiency, calculability, predictability and control; the multiplication of themed spaces, as exemplified by Disneyland, which has produced new opportunities for urban and commercial development; and the confluence of 'form, content and structure' (Hannigan 1998: 81) as once separate activities such as shopping, entertainment and education converge.

In an intriguing merging of the material, imagined and lived, Disney as a culture and a form of built space has found direct expression in the towns and suburbs of America. Sharon Zukin (1997: 49) describes Disney as 'the alter ego and collective fantasy of American society'. For many, the landscape of Disney is one of coherence, imagination and security. Disney speaks to America's (imagined) past and 'a public culture of civility and security that recalls a world long left behind. There are no guns here, no homeless people, no illegal drink or drugs' (Zukin 1997: 52). The spaces of Disney reference real cities and urban spaces at the same time as sanitizing and reconfiguring them. Zukin goes on to examine the ways in which Disney has influenced city building, with festival marketplaces and shopping malls being two that readily come to mind, but the influence is broader and more insidious, infiltrating the service sector, the cultural economy and urban planning. In the view of many, aspects of the influential 'new urbanism' movement that commenced in the United States in the 1980s owe much to the Disney formula, especially its overt referencing of traditional forms of planning and design, including ' "[r]etro" architectural features like porches and dormers' (Grant 2006: 101). New urbanism also focuses on non-car environments and forms of mobility, in particular pedestrianization, public transport and cycling. High-profile examples of new urbanism and its blending of the imagined and the real, the present and the past, are Seaside in Florida, which was the location for the 1998 Peter Weir film *The Truman Show*, Poundbury in the United Kingdom, which has been dubbed the 'town that Charles built' because of having been constructed according to the urban design principles espoused by Prince Charles on land owned by his Duchy of Cornwall (Hardy 2006), and Celebration in Florida, which was in fact developed by the Disney Corporation (MacCannell 2004).

Before Disneyland there were the World Fairs, Expos and Olympic Games, which continue to be major (albeit temporary) incursions into urban landscapes and which frequently are now used as the impetus for significant urban redevelopment. Much is made of the legacy of such events, with the built legacy being central. As temporary urban theme parks, however, World Fairs and Expos have variously been described as celebrations of industrialism, opportunities for cultural display and exchange, and, most recently, exercises in national and city promotion and branding. It is certainly the case that the pavilions of participating nations at the 2010 Shanghai World Expo were overwhelmingly concerned with promoting national identity along with fostering national trade and tourism interests. Central to this agenda was the architecture of the pavilions as well as the content of their exhibitions – it is noteworthy, for instance, that the Egyptian Pavilion was designed by the celebrity/star architect Zaha Hadid. Expos are also noted for creating urban landmarks, such as the Eiffel Tower, which was built for the 1889

World's Fair and is now a globally recognized symbol of the city of Paris (see Chapter 6).

Although most Expo structures, including the pavilions, are dismantled at the end of the event, the example of the Eiffel Tower points to what have from the beginning been important aspects of hosting a World Expo – the fate of the Expo site after the event, and the nature and purpose (both symbolic and material) of any permanent Expo structures. There is now a strong expectation that staging a World Expo will contribute to furthering the entwined cultural, symbolic and urban goals of the host city. Indeed, it has become increasingly common for World Expos to be located on former industrial sites and for the event to be staged either as a high-profile trigger for the subsequent redevelopment of the site or as a key element in a broader regeneration strategy for the area which, more often than not, is focused on pro-viding spaces for cultural and recreational activities, as well as housing. So although the national marketing and eco-nomic agenda has certainly come to dominate the discourses of World Expos – the so-called 'economic Olympics' – this ascendancy has occurred in the context of a complex and extremely enduring local agenda that is focused on using the event to create a positive built legacy.

In an overt confluence of spectacles, the largest shopping mall in Europe opened in September 2011 in East London adjacent to the mega complex of the 2012 Olympic Games site. The Olympics and the Westfield mega-shopping mall are key elements of a broader strategy to redevelop this rundown area of London. Indeed, Westfield Stratford City is described on the official 'Stratford: London' website as being 'one of the largest urban regeneration projects ever undertaken in Europe' as well as the 'gateway to Olympic Park' (http://www.stratfordlondon.info/developments/stratford-city, accessed May 2012). Esther Addley (2011: np), writing in the daily UK newspaper *The Guardian*, describes the 'gateway' function as follows: 'In all, for 70% of visitors, the entrance to the Olym-pics will be through the vast shopping development. Welcome to London 2012? Welcome to Westfield first.'

The London Olympics site is 2.5 square kilometres of what is described as former 'industrial, contaminated land' that has been 'transformed into the largest urban park created in

7.3   Stratford Westfield sign, London, UK.

Europe for more than 150 years' (quoted in Rowe 2008: 403). Olympic Park combines features such as 'riverside gardens, markets, events, cafés and bars' and 'quieter public space and habitats for hundreds of existing and rare species' as well as the landmark sporting venues, including the Olympic Stadium and the (Zaha Hadid-designed) Aquatic Centre (http://www.london2012.com/games/olympic-park/index.php,    accessed April 2011, quotes no longer online). The mega-event, spectacle shopping and urban redevelopment merge in this global-world city, which, according to some measures, is already the most visited city in the world. In using the Olympic Games as the impetus for urban and social redevelopment, London has joined other recent host cities which have transformed former industrial sites into the location for a mega-event. But when discussing the use of a mega-event to transform a city's landscape and image, it is Barcelona and its staging of the Olympic Games in 1992 that is often cited as exemplary.

  Staged in the context of considerable industrial decline and economic crisis, the Barcelona Olympics is credited with increasing local employment, improving public transport, opening the city up to the coast and providing new and redeveloped urban facilities and infrastructure (Horne and Manzenreiter 2006). The urban redevelopment undertaken for the Barcelona Olympics was on a substantial scale and included:

> a new waterfront and residential area ... a new international airport, two new spectacular skyline communications towers (the Colserollo tower at Tibidabo, designed by notable architect Norman Foster, and the Calatrava tower near the Olympic Stadium on Mon Juic), six new sports stadia together with a major refurbishment of the main stadium, a new museum of contemporary art and a remodelled Catalonian arts museum, various media facilities .... (Roche 2000: 145)

This rebuilding came at considerable public expense – 'at least $8 billion ... more than most Olympics have ever cost' (Roche 2000: 145) – and while employment was created, there is evidence to suggest that much of it was low-paid and short-term (Horne and Manzenreiter 2006). It is also possible to ponder the robustness of the built legacy of the Games – the waterfront development, for instance, is a generic themed festival marketplace and much of the infrastructure and many of the buildings and public spaces built or redeveloped for the Games have become rather rundown and ill kempt in the years since the event. Indeed, it is the Gaudí buildings, which predate the Olympics, that are iconic and continue to impress visitors to the city. Nevertheless, the Games played a major part in establishing Barcelona as a leading tourism and conference destination and its experience has influenced many non-world or global cities to bid to host a mega-event such as the Olympics, although few have successfully repositioned the brand of the host city in quite the same way. The Olympic Games is a brand and the Olympic City is branded through its staging of the event. According to Donald and Gammack (2007: 47), not only is staging an Olympic Games intended to strengthen the image of the host city, but also 'each Olympic city strengthens the Olympic brand'. It is noteworthy in this context that the website for the London Olympics has a specific heading entitled 'Our Brand' (http://www.london2012.com/about-us/our-brand/, accessed May 2012). According to this site, the London 2012 brand is 'fundamental to the Games. It is how we identify the Games, how we communicate our ambition, and how we drive excitement and enthusiasm for the Games.'

The language is inclusive, speaking to themes of the insider and shared ambition. Central to the London 2012 brand is a logo or 'emblem', which supposedly combines the city of London (represented by '2012') and the Olympic rings, which are linked through the staging of the Olympics with such qualities as 'confidence, certainty and opportunity'. Importantly, these qualities have little to do with the sporting event but are concerned with place image, tourism and financial investment.

Bidding for, and staging, mega-events such as the Olympic Games usually requires the involvement of different levels of government because they are now major exercises in central planning and public funding. Jon Coaffee (2008) argues that, in the United Kingdom, the attempts to regenerate large urban areas have gone 'hand-in-hand' with the (so-called) 'modernization of the state'. Hosting an event of the scale of the Olympic Games is usually the prerogative of already privileged cities of the West, although the 2014 FIFA World Cup is to be staged in Brazil, Beijing staged the Olympic Games in 2008, and Shanghai the 2010 World Expo. Both China and Brazil, however, are emerging as global economic powerhouses. It is less common for developing cities and nations that are not experiencing significant economic growth to seek to stage such events. Nevertheless, even these cities are not shielded from the processes of masterplanning and visioning which have become central to the urban, economic and social agenda of many cities.

## City visioning for community development

As the world becomes increasingly globalized, neoliberal and urbanized, questions about the way in which cities are managed and urban development priorities set have become urgent. At the same time, many have pointed to the relevance of various intersections of the local, national and global in the building and management of cities – particularly those that are socially, environmentally and economically sustainable. At the global level, state and non-state transnational agencies such as FIFA, the International Olympic Committee, the European Union and the United Nations are in very different ways setting important aspects of the urban development agenda, sometimes through direct funding schemes but also indirectly through priority setting and the influential role they play in the circulation of knowledge about cities and their futures.

An outcome of the 1944 Bretton Woods accord was the establishment of the International Monetary Fund (IMF) and the World Bank, two institutions that play significant roles in influencing global processes of urbanization and the production of space, notably in developing countries. The operations of the World Bank are particularly important as this body is explicitly charged with the task of providing finance to assist developing nations build their physical, social and financial infrastructure. Indeed, Jennifer Robinson (2006) suggests that it was a 1991 initiative of the World Bank that was pivotal in shifting the perception of developing cities as 'drains on the national economy' to being regarded as the 'engines of economic growth'. This repositioning 'emphasised enabling and partnership strategies for housing and services provision (as opposed to state or donor provision) and highlighted the importance of infrastructure provision and efficient city-wide managerial capacity as essential to support economic enterprise' (Robinson 2006: 124). The result has commonly been the formation of trans-sectorial coalitions and the formulation of overarching urban development strategies and visions that are explicitly designed to be combined as part of the urban agenda with the goals of attaining economic growth and ameliorating poverty.

Influential in this context is the Cities Alliance, which is a multi-agency partnership involving the World Bank, UN-HABITAT, a number of national governments and international associations of local authorities. The Cities Alliance has two key concerns: to address the growth of urban slums and effectively to manage those cities where slum growth is taking place (http://www.citiesalliance.org/ca/about-cities-alliance, accessed May 2012). A key mechanism to aid in the achievement of these outcomes is the use of formal city development strategies (CDSs), which are defined on the Alliance's website as being 'an action-oriented process, developed and sustained through participation to promote equitable growth in cities and their surrounding regions to improve the quality of life for all citizens'. To this end, CDSs are intended to be at once strategic and long-term, helping cities to develop the local capacity and processes to allocate resources effectively; attract footloose capital (and 'discipline its use'); build strategic partnerships; plan for urban growth (including determining necessary infrastructure); anticipate 'future shocks'; and clarify the 'vision' that is the future of the city. In other words, the emphasis is on resources, partnerships, cities and the future. Plans, visions and processes.

Robinson (2006: 126–7) describes CDSs as a form of city visioning that pivots on fostering participation and inclusiveness, 'build[ing] an approach to cities that requires a city-wide view and engages with the complexity and diversity of the city'. The Cities Alliance website goes on to detail the five recurring 'themes' that 'successful cities' have 'dealt with' through the CDS process: livelihood, defined in terms of job creation, skills development and entrepreneurialism; environmental quality, service delivery and energy efficiency; urban form and infrastructure development; managing financial resources, with the focus here being on the role and capacity of local government; and, finally, governance, which is seen in terms of coordinating the responsibilities and activities of different levels of government, and of disparate local governments across a single metropolitan region. The illustrative project descriptions provided come from a number of different cities, and underline the focus on the local and the acquisition of knowledge and information. There are also fairly modest initiatives and visions – no place for mega-events under this scheme. The CDS process is not, however, presented as seeking to achieve 'soft' or 'easy' outcomes, as part of the wording of the aim 'to clarify' reveals: '[A] CDS is designed to shock the system under controlled conditions and catalyse new thinking about the city's future.' The use of the word 'shock' in this example is telling and not a one-off – indeed, its recurrence on the website is noteworthy.

There are a number of intriguing connections and assumptions here, including, in particular, the assertion of the importance of the local, both as a (formal and informal) system and structure of government and governance, and as the realm of the urban. According to Robinson (2006: 127), a significant consequence of the changes in the context of urban development that have occurred internationally since the 1990s has been the 'globalisation of local government' as cities increasingly have become entangled in the agendas of national and transnational bodies and the circuits of information and expertise that they foster. Not only is the local central, but it is also frequently regarded as a measure of success. Robinson argues that the CDSs programme of the Cities Alliance was developed in this context in part to give local government the skills to manage changed meta-policy circumstances. What is significant is that the CDSs are underpinned by 'an inclusive and participatory approach to city-visioning' (Robinson 2006: 130) which may be difficult (perhaps impossible) to achieve in practice but, nevertheless, in Robinson's view, marks an important repositioning of city visioning that succumbs neither to developmentalist prescription nor to the allure of global solutions, such as seeking status as a 'world' or 'global' city.

Visioning thus ideally involves imagining an urban future that has been shaped, and is widely shared, by local residents – it is the values and priorities of residents which should inform the vision that is implemented. In the case of the CDSs, the context is clearly global and multi-sectoral, but the strategy and processes are intended to be local. What this example also points to, though, are the complex practices of local planning and associated consultative processes as they are played out in all cities, not only those of developing nations caught very directly in the global web of inter-agency initiatives and priorities. A number of challenges must be addressed when considering how visioning can be made inclusive in the sense, following Robinson's prescription, of being city-wide and engaged. Also relevant is what community or citizen engagement means more generally in urban planning, including in city reimaging and branding. In this context, it is unremarkable but important to observe that most mega-events staged and mega and themed landscapes constructed in Western cities under conditions of globalization, neoliberalism and the operation of powerful economic and political interests occur with little community consultation, let alone engaged participation (Stevenson 1998).

In the decade following 1968, however, many spheres of government in the West demonstrated a surge of interest in the twin ideals of 'community' and 'participation' and asserted their relevance to urban policy and planning. At that time, public pressure and widespread dissatisfaction with established urban development procedures, as well as with their built outcomes, had shaped the view that the facilitation of local community participation held the key to creating more sensitive and democratic processes that would lead ultimately to building more 'liveable' cities (Montgomery and Thornley 1990). An increase in participatory practices was seen as one way of ensuring that decision-making was inclusive and representative. As a result of what was often considerable pressure, sometimes manifested in social movements and urban protests, many governments moved to incorporate 'community interests' into their urban development processes in some way. The emergence of neoliberalism as the dominant discourse in urban development and the processes of entrepreneurial governance it fosters, however, have led, if not to a weakening of obligations to community participation in urban development and reimaging, then certainly to its reconceptualization. These changes are seen by many urban commentators as indicative of a considerable decrease in the influence which local residents now have in shaping the city as a result of an increase in the power of economic over social arguments. Mega-projects, brandscapes, and the like, are routinely the result of top-down processes and the objects of masterplans. There are few, if any, opportunities under these circumstances for a broad range of local interests to influence urban development at the point at which the priorities are set. Rather, community consultation is usually set up to be reactive rather than proactive, focused on collecting responses to a specific masterplan or vision once it has already been developed/proposed. Differences of access to the urban development agenda, therefore, can be very marked, as can differences in the nature of the discursive strategies employed by particular groups at particular times to justify urban proposals.

The devolution of power to local communities, nevertheless, continues to be seen by some as an important way of shaping urban development processes that are more equitable, and of raising the quality of urban life. That said, the devolution of power to communities and collectives is often advocated unchallenged with little or no consideration given to the representativeness of so-called 'community' groups, or to the practices of inclusion and exclusion by which these groups define their constituency and objectives. Urban re-development and notions of 'community participation' and action are splintered, multifaceted struggles over both the structure and the meaning of the built environment. To a considerable extent, too, calls for participation and consultation are often idealistic, pivoting on a nostalgic view of past participation processes. Not all community organizations and categories of social actors within society are equal in city visioning and consultation processes, nor are their objectives those which necessarily take account of, or are compatible with, other perspectives. Incorporating a multiplicity of interests into any urban visioning or development process is extremely difficult. As Patric de Villiers (1997) points out, there is no blueprint detailing how a complete restructuring of urban planning practice and policy might be achieved. But there may still be a strong case for trying to frame a new model for understanding participation in city visioning and masterplanning, which is what Robinson argues could well be occurring in relation to the CDSs community processes.

Ronan Paddison (2001b: 202), too, is keen not to give up on either the notion of community or the possibility of establishing effective participatory procedures in urban redevelopment projects. The starting point, he suggests, is to recognize that communities are political and highly fractured, and, rather than succumbing to the loudest voice or most organized interest groups, to try to develop ways of working with this diversity through participation processes that are engaged, multi-dimensional and protracted – a new vision for visioning perhaps. Still relevant, though, is Leonie Sandercock's (1994a) sobering observation that community consultation is always limited, often ineffective and serves (either by default or design) the interests of those who already control the urban agenda. The key question remains: 'Who has power, and how much of it are they prepared to hand over to the participation process?' (Sandercock 1994b: 7).

## Conclusion

The concern of this chapter was to consider some of the conceptualizations of the city and urbanism that come into view
as a result of overarching visioning processes including city
reimaging and branding. At the centre of such approaches is
a coherent but partial view of the city, its past, present and
future. Such views are intended to be highly marketable and
packaged to bring economic, social and cultural benefits to the
city. Place marketing and city imaging strategies aim to sell the
city or aspects thereof to investors, tourists and residents alike.
Notions of the entrepreneurial city, the city as a growth
machine and entrepreneurial governance are each important
to understanding the processes and orientation of city marketing and imaging. The chapter also discussed the increasingly
important role of branding to these strategies, but, as was
pointed out, branding is more than marketing. The city may
be configured as a brand and represented through slogans, but
brands are now also central elements of the urban landscape
and experience. The spaces of many cities are dominated by
brands, including signage, 'signature' buildings and flagship
stores – the 'wow factor' has become the buzzword, but the
result may well be universality and cliché.

Seriality, theming and standardization are often the flip
side of the quest for the spectacular and the different. So,
too, are marginalization and exclusion as the local and the
idiosyncratic are eschewed in favour of the predictable and
the global. The role of local communities in setting the urban
development and research agenda is thus a vexed one not
only in the city-building projects of the West, but increasingly
in developing cities which look to city visioning as a way to
ameliorate poverty and foster economic growth. And where
the mega-projects of the West eschew local communities, the
success of visioning in the context of disadvantage depends
on the local and the shared. The chapter concluded with a
consideration of some of the complexities of consultation,
suggesting that 'blueprints' or 'strategies' for consultation
are, by definition, partial – the outcomes of imbalances of
power and influence.

# 8
## Conclusion

## Concepts of the City and Beyond

> Each generation, it seems, defines the urban question after its own fashion, as an articulation of social challenges, political predicaments and theoretical issues reflecting the current conjuncture of urban society . . . .
>
> Scott and Moulaert 1997: 267

The starting point for this book – to consider the city as a key concept in contemporary social science – appears straightforward. This is the 'what is the city?' question, which has long vexed many within urban studies, and although, as Scott and Moulaert assert in the passage quoted above, it – and the 'urban question' more broadly – is framed in terms of the issues of the age, the challenge has been to understand 'the city' (and its spatiality) as a social institution that is simultaneously separate from, but shaped by, the processes that comprise society as a whole. Urban sociologists and urban theorists more broadly have thus conceptualized the city in different ways, emphasizing various aspects of urbanism and the urban condition. What unites them is their concern with the social, or 'sociospatial', and an acceptance that there is 'something', however ill defined, about 'the city' that makes it an important and appropriate object of analysis. What also joined many of the early urban sociologists was an acceptance that it was possible to develop an all-encompassing theory that would explain the city and urban life either as a totality or in terms of overarching processes. The city of urban sociology for much of the twentieth century was, therefore, understood in terms of generalizations and classifications. And while the Chicago School was concerned to theorize the structure and nature of the city from observations and other empirical data, Marxist urban researchers were interested in identifying causal relationships between the city and society, and in this regard their focus was on class struggle and the forces and relations of capitalism.

The implicit assumption was that there is a coherent urban question, and that urban processes and explanations of the urban are universally applicable. The concept of 'the city' suggests a unity, just as the associated notions of 'urbanization' and 'urbanism' reference coherent systems. It is clear, however, that neither implication is sustainable and, as a result, many important explanations must be regarded as being partial at best. There is, for instance, little conceptual room within influential accounts focused on the systems, processes and institutions of the city and city building to deal effectively with the structures and experiences of difference, contingency and idiosyncrasy that exist within and between cities. Also frequently ignored are the cities, urban processes and ways of seeing located outside the Anglo-American metropole. The 'what is the city?' question cannot be answered simply or with reference to a single set of theories and assumptions. It must be recast, and at issue is not the concept of the city *per se*, but a range of different questions that urban researchers now ask about cities and urban life and the theories, methods and concepts they bring to this task.

Modern cities are the spaces and surfaces of buildings, roads and infrastructure as well as of everyday life, memory and imagination. Under capitalism, cities are produced through the processes and struggles of capital accumulation and class division. But these macro processes and overarching systems do not determine the everyday or the imagined dimensions of the city and urbanism, and just as the micro cannot be explained with reference to the macro, the micro does not explain the macro. The 'urban question' must be framed in terms of the interplay of both – as simultaneously material (in the sense of structures, processes and built infrastructure), imagined (conceptual and representational) and lived (experienced and sensory). It was suggested in the book that the work of Henri Lefebvre was useful in this respect. Lefebvre regarded the 'production of space' as a three-dimensional process comprised of material (perceived) space, ideological/representational (conceived) space and symbolic (lived) space, which can be analysed separately and in terms of their intersections. He also sought to engage with the multiscalar and historical dimensions of the urban. The task of this book was not to apply Lefebvre's framework to 'the city', but to use key insights as starting or enabling points from which to consider how various dimensions of cities have been understood and engaged with, both separately and in tension, at diverse levels of conceptualization and through oft-competing theoretical lenses. Lefebvre's work, therefore, was introduced as an orientation from which to recognize the multiplicity and multidimensionality of cities and urban space, and the processes and relations that shape and connect them. It is a useful tool in reframing the 'what is the city?' question.

The aim of this book, therefore, was to take the concept of the city and, with reference to a range of urban and socio-logical theories, explore the different ways in which cities (and parts and times thereof) are conceptualized. This objective, and the impossibility of capturing a multifaceted and contested object within a single theoretical framework, led me to adopt an approach that has become quite common within urban studies, and that is to consider aspects of the city and urban life through a series of organizing lenses that render the city metaphorical, but at the same time provide a useful way of engaging with the subject matter. The utilization of frames, including 'globalization', 'materi-ality', 'temporality' and 'emotions', made it possible to look at the various ways in which the city has been studied, the questions that have been asked about cities and urban life, and the sets of explanations that have been applied to dif-ferent aspects of the urban question. The book, therefore, did not attempt to be exhaustive, nor did it trace a history of urban thought – there are numerous urban studies books, readers and encyclopaedias that attempt to do this. Rather, what it did was to engage with and explain some of the most important and contested urban trends and processes and their conceptualization at different levels of spatiality and in terms of recurring themes, such as inequality, homogeneity, rhythm and heterogeneity.

Capitalism in all its forms has been influential in the building and rebuilding of urban environments since the nineteenth century. Indeed, the term 'capitalist city' is one that is frequently coined by those seeking to examine these processes and their built outcomes. Marxist urban researchers regard the capitalist relations of production as both the motor and context of urbanization – determining the physical, cultural and social organization and structure of the city. As discussed in the book, the landscapes of capitalism are those of extremes, of division and inequality, wealth and poverty, consumption and production, degradation and spectacle. Marxism has informed studies of uneven urban development, the distribution of urban resources, and the role of the state in supporting or facilitating capitalism and its urban social relations. Such studies continue to be influential and provide important insights. In its crudest forms, however, Marxism is vulnerable to accusations that it privileges class and the circulation and location of capital over not only the micro and the symbolic, but also other important elements of structuration, including gender, ethnicity and race. Accordingly, many have sought to widen and deepen the concerns of Marxism, with the work of David Harvey and Henri Lefebvre in different ways being influential. Feminists, too, have also challenged and reconceptualized Marxist urban studies.

What Marxism brings to the study of cities and urbanization, however, are valuable insights into the ways in which capital accumulation and investment influence urban growth and the spatial patterning of inequality, including the divisions that form between cities and the development within them of ghettoes and enclaves of wealth, poverty, race and ethnicity. Important have been analyses of what is termed the second circuit of capital, which reveal how capital is attracted away from the primary circuit (production) and into housing and real estate markets, and the social, economic and urban consequences of this shift, including the rise of the finance and investment sector to a position of global economic dominance. As discussed in Chapter 2, the forming of speculative (often unsustainable) property/ housing 'bubbles' is one result of the dominance of financial capitalism; another is the emergence of cities, in particular London and New York, as centres of global finance and investment. The processes of gentrification and of neoliberalism and the notion of the 'neoliberal city' are also important in this context, as are the processes of industrialization and urbanization occurring in developing nations, including China, and their linkages to the global economy.

A concern with the urban geography of inequality, and the role of capitalism and its urban processes in creating it, has prompted an associated interest in what is sometimes conceptualized as the interplay of heterogeneity and homogeneity. Indeed, cities are both celebrated and denigrated for the diversity of their populations, with many urban researchers focusing on the use, regulation and provision of urban public space – streets, parks and civic facilities – in order to understand both the nature of diversity and its potential role in creating enlivened and more democratic cities. For some, the combination of lived diversity and animated public space is essential to the formation of a vibrant civic culture, and to this end a raft of prescriptions have been developed in recent years which serve as blueprints for coalitions of interests keen to nurture particular forms of urbanism and public life. Many of these proposals are highly critical of increased privatization and the degradation of those public spaces which, they argue, historically have been central to a city's culture and identity.

In addition to being implicated in creating the conditions for diversity, the same processes can prompt the development of discrete residential or dormitory zones located away from the city centre and the places of work and industry. These are the suburbs, which are often regarded as the 'other' of the city, variously vilified and embraced for their real and imagined demographic homogeneity and conformity and the social relations they foster. As the form of the city changes, however, the status and shape of the suburbs have also changed. Indeed, the suburbs have become increasingly complex, home to diverse populations as well as being the locations of work, creativity and multifaceted everyday social life. As a result, the influential core–periphery model of the city and the suburb has become difficult to sustain. The twin notions of the 'urbanization of the suburbs' and the 'suburbanization of the city' are more than slogans – they point to very tangible and highly significant changes to urban form and challenges to conceptualizations of 'the city'.

Not only are tensions between the city and the suburbs enmeshed in the opposition of homogeneity and heterogeneity, but they are also conceptualized through the rhythms of time, with the city conventionally being imagined as the place of work and the day-time and the suburbs as the spaces of non-working time, the location of home – the place to go to (literally) 'at the end of the day'. Where the suburbs evoke notions of security, community and family, the urban night, and particularly its public spaces, is routinely associated with danger, excitement and transgression. Moves to gentrify the inner city and stimulate leisure and consumption activity have become increasingly common, and such initiatives are often focused on creativity and fostering sanitized forms of diversity. These efforts, however, point again to the complexity and contradictions of the city. Indeed, attempts to make the city a site of middle-class leisure and consumption have often occurred alongside efforts to stimulate a night-time economy that is heavily based on entertainment and alcohol consumption. The result is a monoculture and associated displays of public drunkenness and disorder that are in conflict with the aspirations of middle-class gentrifiers and the visions of sophisticated night spaces conjured by city planners. The ensuing calls for greater regulation of the city after dark and its uses have led to interventions including spatial containment, increased (often private) policing of public space and the implementation of overt and covert forms of surveillance, such as CCTV. While age is a key fault-line defining the shape and use of the night-time economy, gender has emerged as also important, but in highly unexpected and often challenging ways. Women's use of the city at night has traditionally been considered either through the lens of safety and perceptions of vulnerability or as a highly sexualized disruption or threat to social order. But for many young women who are present in the contemporary night-time economy in ever-increasing numbers, the city can be a source of empowerment and pleasure.

The city at night is a site of heightened sensations – of expectation and adventure, as well as of fear and disgust. In turn, the cities of the day and of the suburbs prompt different sets of emotional responses and engagements. Cities and their spaces are meaningful at both individual and collective levels. The city has rarely been studied through the lens of the emotions, and yet an understanding of the affective is necessary for any comprehensive explanation of the interplay of the lived, imagined and material. Emotions, both personal and collective, shape and take shape in urban space, and in Chapter 5 the contours of a sociological understanding of this relationship were traced. It was argued that the key is to acknowledge that there can be no social action in the absence of enabling emotions. The lived experience of emotion inclines or predisposes people to action, and an appreciation of this relationship is essential for conceptualizations of the city that are neither reductionist nor constructivist. These will acknowledge, and perhaps attempt to engage with, the range of feelings connected with urban place and the social actions which occur in relation to them. The sentiments aroused by particular places and the meanings people derive from, and attach to, these places can influence the way in which they use and imagine space (fear, pleasure and nostalgia come readily to mind), with the practices of avoidance and protest being highly charged uses of, and engagements with, city spaces. The spatial triggers of memory and emotion can take the built and official form of monument, shrine and memorial, but they can also be unofficial, unmarked and unremarkable. The importance of belief and religion in shaping the built and symbolic landscapes of sentiment was also discussed in the book as relevant in this context.

The intersection of memory, imagination and experience is thus manifold and formed through the triadic interplay of the material, imaginative and lived dimensions of space. This is urban space at its most immediate and located, but, as Chapter 6 explained, cities, their images and economies, as well as everyday urban experience, are increasingly defined and made with reference to global networks and flows of capital, people, ideas and services. The city of place and the local is at the same time a city enmeshed in the global. Conceptualizations of the city which come into play in this context include 'global city', 'world city', 'world class city' and a series of league tables, hierarchies and supposed indicators of urban exceptionality and, by implication, mediocrity. Globalization has consolidated the power and wealth of a small number of major cities and locked other cities into seemingly endless competitions for global status and recognition. Globalization thus does not transcend the urban. Rather, the global makes, is made and lived in the spaces of cities. Cities are at the core of the global, and the urban consequences of globalization and the global consequences of urbanization are profound, taking form both within and between cities. Indeed, even rich and prosperous cities contain within them the forgotten sites of poverty, while the division between major cities such as London and New York and other cities within their nation states has become a gulf.

The 'global city and the rest' forms a dichotomy and set of urban consequences that geographers and sociologists have been keen to understand. For instance, British locality studies examined the local politico-economic strategies that were developed in specific (non-metropolitan) cities in response to significant economic change resulting in part from globalization. These studies provided valuable and nuanced insights into the intersection of the global and the local, focusing on the economic, social and political. What would contribute to such understandings are engaged ethnographies of urban life under conditions of globalization, which could reveal the lived dimensions and experiences of (and in) place, as they are formed in the context of global processes of 'othering'. Understanding the emotions and the structures of feeling and meaning that tie people to cities, their homes and neighbourhoods at times of considerable economic and social change is an important aspect of such a task.

Some cities prosper under conditions of neoliberalism and globalization, but many, notably those that are 'industrial', 'developing' and 'regional', are rendered 'other' and come to be defined in terms of (real and imagined) deficit or lack. In response, commentators have argued that a new way of conceptualizing cities is required which recognizes and works with the complexity and diversity of all cities and does not privilege the wealthy cities of the global North. For Jennifer Robinson, for instance, this means bringing the plurality of cities into a single field of analysis through the lens of the 'ordinary city'. The first task in achieving this aim is to uncouple conceptualizations of urbanization and urbanism from the themes and assumptions of modernity and progress. This approach is compelling but difficult to achieve given the dominance not only of 'global' and 'world' cities but also of the discourses associated with them and the ways in which they have come to shape the ambitions of cities to attract capital investment and the 'creative class'. The proliferation of city reimaging and branding schemes that are explicitly designed to speak to the global and the modern is convincing testimony.

City imaging and branding flourish as local politicians and economic interests seek to find ways of packaging and selling their city to visitors, businesses and local communities alike, and to gain a position somewhere on the league tables of cities. As discussed in Chapter 7, the city of visioning (including masterplanning, place marketing and branding) pivots on conceptualizations of a city's real and imagined past, present and future that are coherent but necessarily partial – 'the city' of the brand is one that is summarized, abbreviated. A single, definable city transcends and flattens local complexity. Mega-projects and events are often central elements of a reimaging agenda, but these initiatives are invariably top-down with community consultation and involvement being recast as managing community expectations and defusing opposition. As city visioning increasingly is incorporated into urban social development agendas, however, particularly in the cities of the global South, some have explored the potential of approaches that are participatory, inclusive and achieved through a strong engagement with 'the local'. To this end, a rethinking of power and community, as well as the city, is required. Highly relevant here is Zygmunt Bauman's challenge to reclaim community first by identifying what it might mean in a 'world of individuals' and under conditions of globalization and urbanization. Bauman's suggestion that the way forward may be to reconceptualize community in terms of an ethic of care and shared social responsibility has implications for imaginings of the city because the urban has long been regarded as the antithesis, indeed destroyer, of community.

Among the questions that arise from the concerns of this book are those relating both to the future of the city and to the emerging priorities of urban research. There are two themes that I want to single out. The first is the issue of sustainability – ecological, economic, social and cultural. The 'sustainable city' is not a cliché and can no longer be thought of as an oxymoron. The need for a research agenda that seeks to understand what the city and urban life mean in the context of global warming is perhaps obvious. Also obvious is the need to develop a research strategy and set of explanatory frameworks that are capable of understanding megacities and their environmental implications. But there are other less manifest concerns, including the social, urban and environmental consequences of the proliferation of cultural waste – 'e-waste' – as the cities of the global South become dumping grounds for the obsolete technology of those of the North. These issues require exploration at the interface of disciplines and in ways that consider urbanism in the global North and its consequences for the cities and societies of the global South. The depletion of the world's stocks of fossil fuel is another issue that cuts across social, economic, environmental and global concerns and requires new ways of conceptualizing, building and living in cities. Clearly, urban studies and the disciplines which comprise the field have important roles to play in developing this knowledge and providing a robust research base for policy.

The second theme in the emerging urban research agenda relates to examinations of the ways in which technology is reconfiguring contemporary cities and the nature of urban life. At stake is the role that technology plays in framing new forms of sociality as well as reshaping economies, work and leisure and the spaces within which these activities occur. Not only is technology one of the major fault-lines dividing the cities and nations of the North from those of the global South, but the technological divide is evident also within the cities and neighbourhoods of the North. Access to technology has become a key marker and consequence of urban poverty and inequality, and research that addresses these divisions is important and urgent.

There is no definitive answer to the question 'what is the city?', and yet 'the city' lingers as a concept both in urban studies and in the popular imagination. Indeed, the possibility of conceptualizing 'the city' has implicitly and explicitly informed urban research for more than a century and it also underpins the work of a range of professionals, including urban planners and designers. Engaging with the resonance, underpinning assumptions and contradictions of the concept thus remains an important task for urban scholarship. The aim of this book was to make a modest contribution to this endeavour by probing some of the ways in which the city is conceptualized and with reference to which explanatory frames. The book also contributes to an understanding of the city as comprised of a multiplicity of physical, conceptual and experiential spaces that are shaped through a range of intersecting forces and processes. It is only by proceeding thus that it becomes possible to transcend conceptual divisions and dichotomies and establish the foundations of a nuanced understanding of the urban in its lived, conceived and material complexity.

# References

Abu-Lughod, J. (1987) The Islamic city – historic myth, Islamic essence, and contemporary relevance. *International Journal of Middle East Studies* 19(2), 155–76.

Addley, E. (2011) Welcome to London 2012. But first take a walk through the shopping centre. *The Guardian*, 19 August, http://www.guardian.co.uk/sport/2011/aug/19/london-2012-regeneration-westfield-stratford-city (accessed May 2012).

Amin, A. and Graham, S. (1997) The ordinary city. *Transactions of the Institute of British Geographers* 22(4), 411–29.

Amin, A. and Thrift, N. (1992) Neo-Marshallian nodes in global networks. *International Journal of Urban and Regional Research* 16(4), 571–87.

Amin, A. and Thrift, N. (2008) *Cities: Reimagining the Urban.* Cambridge: Polity.

Anderson, E. (1999) *The Code of the Street.* New York: Norton.

Anderson, N. (1923) *The Hobo.* Chicago: University of Chicago Press.

Appelrouth, S. and Edles, L. (2008) *Classical and Contemporary Sociological Theory.* Los Angeles: Pine Forge Press.

Ashworth, G. and Voogd, H. (1990) *Selling the City: Marketing Approaches in Public Sector Urban Planning.* London: Belhaven.

Bagguley, P., Mark-Lawson, J., Shapiro, D., Urry, J., Walby, S. and Warde, A. (1990) *Restructuring: Place, Class and Gender.* London: Sage.

Bailey, L. (2011) Tales of the cities: results of the Knight Frank Global Cities Survey, http://www.knightfrank.com/wealthreport/2011/global-cities-survey/ (accessed May 2012).

Barbalet, J. (1998) *Emotions, Social Theory and Social Structure: A Macrosociological Approach*. Cambridge: Cambridge University Press.

Barbalet, J. (2002) Introduction: why emotions are crucial. In: J. Barbalet (ed.) *Emotions and Sociology*. Oxford: Blackwell, pp. 1–9.

Barron, J. (2011) China's publicity ads arrive in Times Square. *The New York Times*, 18 January, http://cityroom.blogs.nytimes.com/2011/01/18/chinas-publicity-ads-arrive-in-times-square/ (accessed May 2012).

Bauman, Z. (1994) Desert spectacular. In: K. Tester (ed.) *The Flâneur*. London: Routledge, pp. 138–58.

Bauman, Z. (2011a/2001) *Community: Seeking Safety in an Insecure World*. Cambridge: Polity.

Bauman, Z. (2011b/2000) *Liquid Modernity*. Cambridge: Polity.

Bavinton, N. (2010) Putting leisure to work: city image and representations of nightlife. *Journal of Policy Research in Tourism, Leisure and Events* 2(3), 236–50.

Bavinton, N. (2011) 'To Socialise with Random Strangers . . .': Cultures of Consumption in Night-Time Urban Space. Unpublished Ph.D. thesis, University of Western Sydney, Australia.

Beaumont, J. (2008) Faith action on urban social issues. *Urban Studies* 45(10), 2019–34.

Beaumont, J. and Dias, C. (2008) Faith-based organisations and urban social justice in the Netherlands. *Tijdscrift voor Economische en Sociale Geografie* 99(4), 382–92.

Beauregard, R. (2010) Urban studies. In: R. Hutchison (ed.) *Encyclopedia of Urban Studies*. Thousand Oaks, CA: Sage, pp. 930–5.

Beck, U. (2002) The cosmopolitan society and its enemies. *Theory, Culture and Society* 19(1–2), 17–44.

Bell, C. and Newby, H. (1982) *Community Studies*. London: Allen and Unwin.

Bell, D. and Jayne, M. (2006) Conceptualising small cities. In: D. Bell and M. Jayne (eds.) *Small Cities: Urban Experience beyond the Metropolis*. Milton Park, UK: Routledge, pp. 1–18.

Benjamin, W. (1973) *Charles Baudelaire: A Lyric Poet in the Era of High Capitalism* (translated by H. Zohn). London: New Left Books.

Benjamin, W. (1979) *One Way Street and Other Writings* (translated by E. Jephcott and K. Shorter). London: New Left Books.

Benjamin, W. (1995) Paris: capital of the nineteenth century. In: P. Kasinitz (ed.) *Metropolis: Centre and Symbol of Our Times*. Houndmills, UK: Macmillan, pp. 46–57.

Bennett, T. (2001) *Differing Diversities: Transversal Study on the Theme of Cultural Policy and Cultural Diversity*. Strasbourg: Council of Europe Publishing.

Bianchini, F. (1995) Night cultures, night economies. *Planning Practice and Research* 10(2), 121–6.

Bianchini, F., Fisher, M., Montgomery, J. and Worpole, K. (1988) *City Centres, City Cultures: The Role of the Arts in the Revitalisation of Towns and Cities*. Manchester: Centre for Local Economic Strategies.

Boyd, R. (1968) *Australia's Home: Its Origins, Builders and Occupiers*. Ringwood, Victoria: Pelican.

Boyer, M. (1996) *The City of Collective Memory: Its Historical Imagery and Architectural Entertainments*. Cambridge, MA: MIT Press.

Brabazon, T. and Mallinder, S. (2007) Into the night-time economy: work, leisure, urbanity and the creative industries. *Nebula* 4(3), 161–78.

Brenner, N. and Theodore, N. (2004) Cities and the geographies of 'actually existing neoliberalism'. In: N. Brenner and N. Theodore (eds.) *Spaces of Neoliberalism: Urban Restructuring in North America and Western Europe*. Malden, MA: Blackwell, pp. 2–32.

Brown, J. (1991) How to safeguard London's world city status? *Town & Country Planning* 60, 140–2.

Brown, R. and Gregg, M. (forthcoming) The pedagogy of regret: Facebook, binge drinking and young women. *Continuum: Journal of Media and Cultural Studies*.

Bruno, G. (2002) *Atlas of Emotion: Journeys in Art, Architecture and Film*. London: Verso.

Bryman, A. (1999) The Disneyization of society. *Sociological Review* 47(1), 25–49.

Bryson, L. and Thompson, F. (1972) *An Australian Newtown*. Harmondsworth, UK: Penguin.

Burdett, R. and Rode, P. (2010) The urban age project. In: R. Burdett and D. Sudjic (eds.) *The Endless City*. London: Phaidon, pp. 8–31.

Burdett, R. and Sudjic, D. (eds.) (2010) *The Endless City*. London: Phaidon.

Castells, M. (1972) *The Urban Question*. London: Edward Arnold.

Castells, M. (1991) *The Informational City: Information Technology, Economic Restructuring and the Urban-Regional Process*. Oxford: Basil Blackwell.

Chatterton, P. and Hollands, R. (2002) Theorising urban play-scapes: producing, regulating and consuming youthful nightlife city spaces. *Urban Studies* 39(1), 95–116.

Chatterton, P. and Hollands, R. (2003) *Urban Nightscapes: Youth Cultures, Pleasure Spaces and Corporate Power*. London: Routledge.

Chen, X. (2010) China's new revolution. In: R. Burdett and D. Sudjic (eds.) *The Endless City*. London: Phaidon, pp. 126–33.

Coaffee, J. (2008) Sport, culture and the modern state: emerging themes in stimulating urban redevelopment in the UK. *International Journal of Cultural Policy* 14(4), 377–97.

Coleman, R. (2004) *Reclaiming the Streets: Surveillance, Social Control and the City*. Cullompton, UK: Willan Publishing.

Collis, C., Felton, E. and Graham, P. (2010) Beyond the inner city: real and imagined places in creative place policy and practice. *The Information Society* 26(2), 104–12.

Connell, R. (2010) *Southern Theory: The Global Dynamics of Knowledge in Social Science*. Cambridge: Polity.

Cooke, P. (ed.) (1989) *Localities: The Changing Face of Urban Britain*. London: Unwin Hyman.

Cox, H. (1965) *The Secular City*. New York: Macmillan.

Craven, I. (1995) Cinema, postcolonialism and Australian suburbia. *Australian Studies* 9, 43–70.

Davis, M. (2004) Planet of slums. *New Left Review* 26 (March–April), 5–34.

Davis, M. (2006) *Planet of Slums*. London and New York: Verso.

Davis, M. (1990) *City of Quartz: Excavating the Future in Los Angeles*. London: Vintage.

de Certeau, M. (1988/1980) *The Practice of Everyday Life* (translated by S. Randall). Berkeley: University of California Press.

de Villiers, P. (1997) New urbanism. *The Australian Planner* 34(1), 30–5.

Devine-Glass, F. (1994) 'Mythologising spaces': representing the city in Australian literature. In: L.C. Johnson (ed.) *Suburban Dreaming: An Interdisciplinary Approach to Australian Cities*. Geelong, Victoria: Deakin University Press, pp. 160–80.

Donald, S. H. and Gammack, J. G. (2007) *Tourism and the Branded City: Film and Identity on the Pacific Rim*. Aldershot, UK: Ashgate.

Dovey, K., with Sandercock, L., Stevens, Q., Woodcock, I. and Wood, S. (2005) *Fluid City: Transforming Melbourne's Urban Waterfront*. Sydney: UNSW Press.

Du Bois, W. E. B. (1899) *The Philadelphia Negro*. Philadelphia, PA: University of Pennsylvania Press.

Durkheim, É. (1995/1912) *The Elementary Forms of Religious Life* (translated by K. Fields). New York: Free Press.

Elden, S. (2010) Rhythmanalysis: an introduction. In: H. Lefebvre, *Rhythmanalysis: Space, Time and Everyday Life* (translated by S. Elden and G. Moore). London: Continuum, pp. vii–xv.

Engels, F. (1969/1892) *The Conditions of the Working Class in England.* Frogmore, UK: Panther.

Evans, G. (2001) *Cultural Planning: An Urban Renaissance?* London and New York: Routledge.

Everingham, C. (2003) *Social Justice and the Politics of Community.* Aldershot, UK: Ashgate.

Florida, R. (2003) *The Rise of the Creative Class: And How It's Transforming Work, Leisure, Community and Everyday Life.* London: Basic Books.

Florida, R. (2004) *Cities and the Creative Class.* New York: Routledge.

Florida, R. (2009) How the crash will reshape America. *The Atlantic Magazine*, March, http://www.theatlantic.com/magazine/archive/2009/03/how-the-crash-will-reshape-america/7293/ (accessed May 2012).

Friedmann, J. (1986) The World City hypothesis. *Development and Change* 17(1), 69–83.

Frisby, D. (1986) *Fragments of Modernity: Theories of Modernity in the Work of Simmel, Kracauer and Benjamin.* Cambridge, MA: MIT Press.

Frisby, D. (2007) *Cityscapes of Modernity.* Cambridge: Polity.

Gans, H. (1962) Urbanism and suburbanism as ways of life. In: M. Rose (ed.) *Human Behaviour and Social Process.* London: Routledge and Kegan Paul, London, pp. 625–48.

Gans, H. (1995) Urbanism and suburbanism as ways of life [reprint with postscript]. In: P. Kasinitz (ed.) *Metropolis: Centre and Symbol of Our Times.* Houndmills, UK: Macmillan, pp. 170–95.

Gans, H. (1967) *The Levittowners: Ways of Life and Politics in a New Suburban Community.* New York: Pantheon Books.

Gans, H. (2008) Involuntary segregation and the ghetto: disconnecting process and place. *City and Community* 7(4), 353–7.

Garreau J. (1991) *Edge City: Life on the New Frontier.* New York: Doubleday.

Geddes, P. (1915) *Cities in Evolution.* London: Williams and Norgate.

Giddens, A. (1990) *The Consequences of Modernity.* Cambridge: Polity.

Gidley, J. (2010) Shanghai, People's Republic of China. In: *RMIT University Annual Review 2010 of Global Cities.* Melbourne: Global Cities Institute, RMIT University, pp. 18–27.

Gilloch, G. (1997) *Myth and Metropolis: Walter Benjamin and the City.* Cambridge: Polity.

Glaeser, E. (2011) *Triumph of the City: How our Greatest Invention Makes Us Richer, Smarter, Greener, Healthier, and Happier.* London: Penguin.

Glass, R. (1964) *London: Aspects of Change.* London: MacGibbon and Kee.

Gleeson, B. (2006) *Australian Heartlands: Making Space for Hope in the Suburbs.* Crows Nest, NSW: Allen and Unwin.

Gotham, K. (2009) Creating liquidity out of spatial fixity: the secondary circuit of capital and the subprime mortgage crisis. *International Journal of Urban and Regional Research* 33(2), 355–71.

Gottdiener, M. (1985) *The Social Production of Urban Space.* Austin: University of Texas Press.

Gottdiener, M. (1997) *The Theming of America: Dreams, Visions and Commercial Spaces.* Boulder, CO: Westview Press.

Gottdiener, M. and Hutchison, R. (2006) *The New Urban Sociology*, 3rd edn. Boulder, CO: Westview Press.

Grant, J. (2006) *Planning the Good Community: New Urbanism in Theory and Practice.* Milton Parl, UK: Routledge.

Grant, R. and Nijman, J. (2006) Globalization and the corporate geography of cities in the less-developed world. In: N. Brenner and R. Kell (eds.) *The Global Cities Reader.* London and New York: Routledge, pp. 223–37.

Griffiths, R. (1995) Eurocities. *Planning Practice and Research* 10(2), 215–21.

Grosz, E. (1995) *Space, Time and Perversion: Essays on the Politics of Body.* London: Routledge.

Habermas, J. (1991/1962) *The Structural Transformation of the Public Sphere: An Inquiry into a Category of Bourgeois Society* (translated by T. Burger and F. Lawrence). Cambridge, MA: MIT Press.

Habermas, J. (1996/1992) *Between Facts and Norms* (translated by W. Rehg). Cambridge: Polity.

Habermas, J. (2006) Religion in the Public Sphere. *European Journal of Philosophy* 14(1), 1–25.

Hall, P. (1977/1966) *The World Cities.* London: Weidenfeld and Nicolson.

Hall, P. (1992) *Cities of Tomorrow.* Oxford: Blackwell.

Hall, S. (1993) Culture, community, nation. *Cultural Studies* 7(3), 349–63.

Hall, T. and Hubbard, P. (1998) *The Entrepreneurial City: Geographies of Politics, Regime and Representation.* Chichester, UK: John Wiley and Sons.

Hanley, J. (2007) Where Space Meets Place in the City: Exploring the Relationship between Resident Action and Local Government Participatory Processes. Unpublished Ph.D. thesis, The University of Newcastle, Australia.

Hannigan, J. (1998) *Fantasy City*. London: Routledge.

Hardy, D. (2006) *Poundbury: The Town That Charles Built*. London: Town and Country Planning Association.

Harloe, M., Pickvance, C. and Urry, J. (eds.) (1990) *Place, Policy and Politics: Do Localities Matter?* London: Unwin Hyman.

Harvey, D. (1973) *Social Justice and the City*. London: Edward Arnold.

Harvey, D. (1982) *The Limits to Capital*. Oxford: Blackwell.

Harvey, D. (1987) Three myths in search of a reality in urban studies. *Environment and Planning D: Society and Space 5*, 367–76.

Harvey, D. (1989a) *The Condition of Postmodernity: An Enquiry into the Origins of Cultural Change*. Oxford: Basil Blackwell.

Harvey, D. (1989b) From managerialism to entrepreneurialism: the transformation in urban governance in late capitalism. *Geografiska Annaler. Series B, Human Geography* 71(1), 3–17.

Harvey, D. (1991) Afterword. In: H. Lefebvre, *The Production of Space* (translated by D. Nicholson-Smith). Oxford: Blackwell, pp. 425–34.

Harvey, D. (1992) Social justice, postmodernism and the city. *International Journal of Urban and Regional Research* 16, 588–602.

Harvey, D. (2007) *A Brief History of Neoliberalism*. Oxford: Oxford University Press.

Harvey, D. (2010) *The Enigma of Capital: And the Crises of Capitalism*. London: Profile Books.

Hayden, D. (2004) *A Field Guide to Sprawl*. New York: Norton.

Hayek, F. (2005/1944) *The Road to Serfdom*. London: Routledge.

Haynes, B. and Hutchison, R. (2008) The *Ghetto*: origins, history, discourse. *City and Community* 7(4), 347–52.

Hayward, K. (2004) *City Limits: Crime, Consumer Culture and the Urban Experience*. London: Glasshouse Press.

Heath, T. and Strickland, R. (1997) The twenty-four hour city concept. In: T. Oc and S. Tiesdell (eds.) *Safer City Centres: Reviving the Public Realm*. London: Chapman, pp. 170–83.

Highmore, B. (2005) *Cityscapes: Cultural Readings in the Material and Symbolic City*. Basingstoke and New York: Palgrave Macmillan.

Hobbs, D., Lister, S., Hadfield, P., Winlow, S. and Hall, S. (2000) Receiving shadows: governance and liminality in the night-time economy. *British Journal of Sociology* 51(4), 701–17.

Hobbs, D., Hadfield, P., Lister, S. and Winlow, S. (2002) 'Door lore': the art and economics of intimidation. *British Journal of Criminology* 42(2), 352–70.

Horne, J. and Manzenreiter, W. (2006) An introduction to the sociology of sports mega-events. *The Sociological Review* 54(s2), 1–24.

Howard, E. (1965/1902) *Garden Cities of Tomorrow*. London: Faber and Faber.

Hubbard, P. and Hall, T. (1998) The entrepreneurial city and the new urban politics. In: T. Hall and P. Hubbard (eds.) *The Entrepreneurial City: Geographies of Politics, Regime and Representation*. Chichester, UK: John Wiley and Sons, pp. 1–24.

Institute for Urban Strategies, The Mori Memorial Foundation (2010) Global Power City Index 2010, http://www.mori-m-foundation.or.jp/english/research/project/6/pdf/GPCI2010_English.pdf (accessed May 2012).

Jacobs, J. (1993/1961) *The Death and Life of Great American Cities*. New York: The Modern Library.

Jayne, M., Valentine, G. and Holloway, S. (2011) *(Dis)Orderly Geographies: Alcohol, Drinking, Drunkenness*. Farnham, UK: Ashgate.

Kasinitz, P. (1995) Modernity and the urban ethos: introduction. In: P. Kasinitz (ed.) *Metropolis: Centre and Symbol of Our Times*. Houndmills, UK: Macmillan, pp. 7–20.

Katz, B. and Altman, A. (2010) An urban age in a suburban nation. In: R. Burdett and D. Sudjic (eds.) *The Endless City*. London: Phaidon, pp. 96–103.

Kavaratzis, M. (2004) From city marketing to city branding: towards a theoretical framework for developing city brands. *Place Branding* 1(1), 58–73.

Kearns, G. and Philo, C (eds.) (1993) *Selling Places: The City as Cultural Capital, Past and Present*. Oxford: Pergamon.

King, A. (1990a) *Global Cities: Post-Imperialism and the Internationalization of London*. London: Routledge.

King, A. (1990b) Architecture, capital and the globalization of culture. In: M. Featherstone (ed.) *Global Culture: Nationalism, Globalization and Modernity*. London: Sage, pp. 397–411.

King, A. (1993) Identity and difference: the internationalization of capital and the globalization of culture. In: P. Knox (ed.) *The Restless Urban Landscape*. Englewood Cliffs, NJ: Prentice Hall, pp. 83–103.

Kipfer, S. and Goonewardena, K. (2007) Colonization and the new imperialism: on the meaning of urbicide today. *Theory and Event* 10(2), http://muse.jhu.edu/journals/theory_and_event/toc/tae10.2.html (accessed May 2012).

Kipfer, S., Schmid, C., Goonewardena, K. and Milgrom, R. (2008a) On the production of Henri Lefebvre. In: K. Goonewardena, S. Kipler, R. Milgrom and C. Schmid (eds.) *Space, Difference, Everyday Life: Reading Henri Lefebvre*. New York and Milton Park, UK: Routledge, pp. 1–21.

Kipfer, S., Schmid, C., Goonewardena, K. and Milgrom, R. (2008b) Globalizing Lefebvre? In: K. Goonewardena, S. Kipler, R. Milgrom and C. Schmid (eds.) *Space, Difference, Everyday Life: Reading Henri Lefebvre*. New York and Milton Park, UK: Routledge, pp. 285–301.

Kling, R., Olin, S. and Poster, M. (1995) The emergence of post-suburbia: an introduction. In: R. Kling, S. Olin and M. Poster (eds.) *Postsuburban California: The Transformation of Orange County since World War II*. Berkeley and Los Angeles: University of California Press, pp. 1–30.

Klingmann, A. (2010) *Brandscapes: Architecture in the Experience Economy*. Cambridge, MA: MIT Press.

Kofman, E. and Lebas, E. (2003) Lost in transportation – time, space and the city. In: E. Kofman and E. Lebas (eds.) *Writing on Cities: Henri Lefebvre*. Malden, MA and Carlton, Victoria: Blackwell, pp. 3–60.

Kozinets, R., Sherry, J., DeBerry-Spence, B., Duhachek, A., Nuttavuthisit, K. and Storm, D. (2002) Themed flagship brand stores in the new millennium: theory, practice, prospects. *Journal of Retailing* 78(1), 17–29.

Landry, C. (2002) *The Creative City: A Toolkit for Urban Innovators*. London: Earthscan.

Landry, C. (2006) *The Art of City Making*. London: Earthscan.

Landry, C. and Bianchini, F. (1995) *The Creative City*. London: Demos.

Lechner, F. (1992) The case against secularization: a rebuttal. *Social Forces* 69(4), 1103–19.

Lefebvre, H. (1991/1974) *The Production of Space* (translated by D. Nicholson-Smith). Oxford: Blackwell.

Lefebvre, H. (2003a/1970) *The Urban Revolution* (translated by R. Bononno). Minneapolis: University of Minnesota Press.

Lefebvre, H. (2003b) No salvation away from the centre? In: E. Kofman and E. Lebas (eds.) *Writings on Cities: Henri Lefebvre* (translated by E. Kofman and E. Lebas). Carlton, Victoria: Blackwell, pp. 205–9.

Lefebvre, H. (2008a/1961) *Critique of Everyday Life Volume 2: Foundations for a Sociology of the Everyday.* London and New York: Verso.

Lefebvre, H. (2008b/1981) *Critique of Everyday Life Volume 3: From Modernity to Modernism.* London and New York: Verso.

Lefebvre, H. (2010/1992) *Rhythmanalysis: Space, Time and Everyday Life* (translated by S. Elden and G. Moore). London: Continuum.

Lefebvre, H. and Régulier, C. (2010/1992) The rhythmanalytical project. In: H. Lefebvre, *Rhythmanalysis: Space, Time and Everyday Life* (translated by S. Elden and G. Moore). London: Continuum, pp. 73–83.

Ley, D. (1980) Liberal ideology and the post-industrial city. *Annals of the Association of American Geographers* 70(2), 238–58.

Logan, J. and Molotch, H. (2007) *Urban Fortunes: The Political Economy of Place.* Berkeley and Los Angeles: University of California Press.

Lovatt, A. and O'Connor, J. (1995) Cities and the night-time economy. *Planning Practice and Research* 10(2), 127–35.

Lukes, S. (1981) *Émile Durkheim: His Life and Work: A Historical and Critical Study.* Harmondsworth, UK: Penguin.

MacCannell, D. (2004) New urbanism and its discontents. In: M. Miles and T. Hall with I. Borden (eds.) *The City Reader*, 2nd edn. Milton Park, UK: Routledge, pp. 382–95.

McDowell, L. (1983) Towards an understanding of the gender division of urban space. *Environment and Planning D: Society and Space* 1(1), 59–72.

McGuigan, J. (2009) Doing a Florida thing: the creative class thesis and cultural policy. *International Journal of Cultural Policy* 15(3), 291–300.

McNeill, D. (2008) *The Global Architect: Firms, Fame and Urban Form.* New York: Routledge.

McNeill, D. (2012) The 'original globalizer'? A spatial ontology of Roman Catholicism. Unpublished paper presented in the Institute for Culture and Society Seminar Series, University of Western Sydney, Australia.

Martin, P. and Rogers, C. (1995) Industrial location and public infrastructure. *Journal of International Economics* 39(3–4), 335–51.

Massey, D. (1991) The political place of locality studies. *Environment and Planning A* 23(2), 267–81.

Massey, D. (2008) *For Space.* London and New York: Sage.

Massey, D. (2011) *World City.* Cambridge: Polity.

Matrix (1984) *Making Space: Women and the Man-Made Environment*. London: Pluto Press.

Miles, M. (1997) *Art, Space and the City: Public Art and Urban Futures*. London and New York: Routledge.

Miller, T. (2012) Culture of creativity to environment – and back again. In: G. Young and D. Stevenson (eds.) *Research Companion to Planning and Culture*. London: Ashgate.

Molotch, H. (1976) The city as a growth machine: toward a political economy of place. *The American Journal of Sociology* 82(2), 309–32.

Monk, J. (1992) Gender in the landscape: expressions of power and meaning. In: K. Anderson and F. Gale (eds.) *Inventing Places: Studies in Cultural Geography*. Melbourne: Longman, pp. 123–38.

Montgomery, J. (1995) The story of Temple Bar: creating Dublin's cultural quarter. *Planning, Practice and Research* 10(2), 135–72.

Montgomery, J. (2008) *The New Wealth of Cities: City Dynamics and the Fifth Wave*. Aldershot, UK: Ashgate.

Montgomery, J. and Thornley, A. (eds.) (1990) *Radical Planning Initiatives: New Dimensions for Urban Planning in the 1990s*. Aldershot, UK: Gower.

Mulgan, G. (1989) The changing shape of the city. In: S. Hall and M. Jacques (eds.) *New Times: The Changing Face of Politics in the 1990s*. London: Lawrence and Wishart, pp. 262–78.

Mumford, L. (1989/1961) *The City in History: Its Origins, Its Transformations, and Its Prospects*. New York: Harcourt.

New South Wales Department of Infrastructure, Planning and Natural Resources (2004) Sydney Metropolitan Strategy – Ministerial Directions Paper. Department of Infrastructure, Planning and Natural Resources, Sydney, NSW.

Nicolaides, B. (2002) *My Blue Heaven: Life and Politics in the Working-Class Suburbs of Los Angeles, 1920–1965*. Chicago: University of Chicago Press.

Oxley, H. (1973) *Mateship in Local Organization*. St Lucia: University of Queensland Press.

Paddison, R. (2001a) Preface. In: R. Paddison (ed.) *Handbook of Urban Studies*. London and New York: Sage, pp. ix–xi.

Paddison, R. (2001b) Communities in the city. In: R. Paddison (ed.) *Handbook of Urban Studies*. London and New York: Sage, pp. 194–205.

Pain, R. (2001) Gender, race, age and fear in the city. *Urban Studies* 38(5–6), 899–913.

Pain, R. and Townshend, T. (2002) A safer city centre for all? Senses of 'Community Safety' in Newcastle upon Tyne. *Geoforum* 33(1), 105–19.

Park, R. (1915) The city: suggestions for the investigation of human behavior in the city environment. *The American Journal of Sociology* 20(5), 557–612.

Pattillo-McCoy, M. (2000) *Black Picket Fences: Privilege and Peril among the Black Middle Class*. Chicago: University of Chicago Press.

Peck, J. (2005) Struggling with the creative class. *International Journal of Urban and Regional Research* 29(4), 740–70.

Phelps, N., Wood, A. and Valler, D. (2010) A postsuburban world? An outline of a research agenda. *Environment and Planning A* 42(2), 366–83.

Pickvance, C. (1990) Introduction: the institutional context of local economic development: central controls, spatial policies and local economic policies. In: M. Harloe, C. Pickvance and J. Urry (eds.) *Place, Policy and Politics: Do Localities Matter?* London: Unwin Hyman, pp. 1–32.

Pirenne, H. (2000) City origins. In: R. T. LeGates and F. Stout (eds.) *The City Reader*. London and New York: Routledge, pp. 38–41.

Rex, J. and Moore, R. (1967) *Race, Community and Conflict: A Study of Sparkbrook*. Oxford: Oxford University Press.

Richards, G. and Palmer, R. (2010) *Eventful Cities: Cultural Management and Urban Revitalization*. London and New York: Butterworth-Heinemann.

Richards, L. (1990) *Nobody's Home: Dreams and Realities in a New Suburb*. Melbourne: Oxford University Press.

Ritzer, G. (1993) *The McDonaldization of Society*. Thousand Oaks, CA: Pine Forge Press.

Ritzer, G. and Liska, A. (1997) 'McDisneyization' and 'post-tourism': complementary perspectives on contemporary tourism. In: C. Rojek and J. Urry (eds.) *Touring Cultures: Transformations of Travel and Theory*. London and New York: Routledge, pp. 96–109.

Robinson, J. (2002) Global and world cities: the view from off the map. *International Journal of Urban and Regional Research* 26(3), 531–54.

Robinson, J. (2006) *Ordinary Cities: Between Modernity and Development*. Milton Park, UK: Routledge.

Roche, M. (2000) *Mega-Events and Modernity: Olympics and Expos in the Growth of Global Culture*. London and New York: Routledge.

190     *References*

Roozen, D.A. (2009) Faith Communities Today 2008: A First Look. Hartford Seminary, Hartford Institute for Religion Research, http://faithcommunitiestoday.org/sites/all/themes/factzen4/files/FACT20081stLook.pdf (accessed May 2012).

Roschelle, A. R. and Wright, T. (2003) Gentrification and social exclusion: spatial policing and homeless activist responses in the San Francisco Bay Area. In: M. Miles and T. Hall (eds.) *Urban Futures: Critical Commentaries on Shaping the City.* London and New York: Routledge, pp. 149–66.

Rowe, D. (2008) Culture, sport and the night-time economy. *International Journal of Cultural Policy* 14(4), 399–415.

Rowe, D. (2011) *Global Media Sport: Flows, Forms and Futures.* London: Bloomsbury Academic.

Rowe, D. (2012) The Shanghai Expo and the Beijing Olympics: image projection and the East Asian mega-event. In: T. Winter (ed.) *Imagined Worlds: China and the Shanghai Expo.* London and New York: Routledge.

Rowe, D. and Baker, S.A. (2012) 'Truly a fan experience'? The cultural politics of the live site. In: R. Krøvel and T. Roksvold (eds.) *We Love to Hate Each Other: Mediated Football Fan Culture.* Gothenburg: Nordicom, pp. 301–17.

Rugh, J. S. and Massey, D. S. (2010) Racial segregation and the American foreclosure crisis. *American Sociological Review* 75(5), 629–51.

Saegert, S. (1980) Masculine cities and feminine suburbs: polarized ideas, contradictory realities. *Signs* 5(3) (supplement), S93–S111.

Sandercock, L. (1994a) With or against the state? In: W. Sarkissian and D. Perlgut (eds.) *Community Participation in Practice: The Community Participation Handbook.* Perth: Institute for Science and Technology Policy, Murdoch University, p. 7.

Sandercock, L. (1994b) Citizen participation: the new conservatism. In: W. Sarkissian and D. Perlgut (eds.) *Community Participation in Practice: The Community Participation Handbook.* Perth: Institute for Science and Technology Policy, Murdoch University, pp. 7–15.

Sandercock, L. (2003) *Cosmopolis II: Mongrel Cities of the 21st Century.* London and New York: Continuum.

Sassen, S. (1991) *The Global City: New York, London, Tokyo.* Princeton: Princeton University Press.

Sassen, S. (2000) A new geography of centers and margins: summary and implications. In: R. T. LeGates and F. Stout (eds.) *The City Reader.* London and New York: Routledge, pp. 208–12.

Sassen, S. (2010a) Public space. In: R. Burdett and D. Sudjic (eds.) *The Endless City.* London: Phaidon, p. 490.

Sassen, S. (2010b) Seeing like a city. In: R. Burdett and D. Sudjic (eds.) *The Endless City.* London: Phaidon, pp. 276–89.

Saunders, D. (2010) *Arrival City: The Final Migration and Our Next World.* Toronto: Knopf Canada.

Savage, M. and Warde, A. (1993) *Urban Sociology, Capitalism and Modernity.* London: Macmillan.

Savage, M., Barlow, J., Duncan, S. and Saunders, P. (1987) 'Locality research': the Sussex programme on economic restructuring, social change and the locality. *Quarterly Journal of Social Affairs* 3(1), 27–51.

Schivelbusch, W. (1988/1983) *Disenchanted Night: The Industrialization of Light in the Nineteenth Century* (translated by A. Davis). Berkeley: University of California Press.

Schmid, C. (2008) Lefebvre's theory of the production of space: towards a three-dimensional dialectic. In: K. Goonewardena, S. Kipler, R. Milgrom and C. Schmid (eds.) *Space, Difference, Everyday Life: Reading Henri Lefebvre.* New York and Milton Park, UK: Routledge, pp. 27–46.

Schutz, A. (2004) Concepts and theory formation in the social sciences. In: C. Seale (ed.) *Social Research Methods: A Reader.* London and New York: Routledge, pp. 211–16.

Scott, A. J. and Moulaert, F. (1997) The urban question and the future of urban research. In: F. Moulaert and A. J. Scott (eds.) *Cities, Enterprises and Society on the Eve of the 21st Century.* London: Pinter, pp. 267–78.

Scott, A., Agnew, J., Soja, E. and Storper, M. (2001) Global city-regions. In: A. Scott (ed.) *Global City-Regions: Trends, Theory, Policy.* Oxford: Oxford University Press, pp. 11–30.

Sennett, R. (1978) *The Fall of Public Man: On the Social Psychology of Capitalism.* New York: Vintage Books.

Sherry, J. (1987) Cereal monogamy: brand loyalty as secular ritual in consumer culture. Unpublished paper presented at 17th Annual Conference of the Association for Consumer Research, Toronto, Canada.

Short, J. (1991) *Imagined Country: Society, Culture and Environment.* London and New York: Routledge.

Simmel, G. (1995) The metropolis and mental life. In: P. Kasinitz (ed.) *Metropolis: Centre and Symbol of Our Times.* London: Macmillan, pp. 30–45.

Skidelsky, R. (2010) *Keynes: The Return of the Master.* London: Penguin.

Smith, N. (1979) Towards a theory of gentrification: a back to the city movement by capital not by people. *Journal of the American Planning Association* 45(4), 538–48.

Smith, N. (1982) Gentrification and uneven development. *Economic Geography* 58(2), 139–55.

Smith, N. (1996) *The New Urban Frontier: Gentrification and the Revanchist City*. London: Routledge.

Soja, E. (1996) *Thirdspace: Journeys to Los Angeles and Other Real and Imagined Places*. Malden, MA: Blackwell.

Sorkin, M. (ed.) (1992) *Variations on a Theme Park: The American City and the End of Public Space*. New York: Hill and Wang.

Stets, J. and Turner, J. (2008) The sociology of emotions. In: M. Lewis, J. Haviland-Jones and L.F. Barrett (eds.) *Handbook of Emotions*. New York: Guilford, pp. 32–46.

Stevenson, D. (1998) *Agendas in Place: Urban and Cultural Planning for Cities and Regions*. Rockhampton: RSERC University of Central Queensland.

Stevenson, D. (1999) Reflections of a 'great port city': the case of Newcastle, Australia. *Environment and Planning D: Society and Space* 17(1), 105–21.

Stevenson, D. (2003) *Cities and Urban Cultures*. Maidenhead, UK and Philadelphia: Open University Press.

Stevenson, D. (2004) 'Civic gold' rush: cultural planning and the politics of the third way. *The International Journal of Cultural Policy* 10(1), 119–31.

Stevenson, D. (forthcoming) *Cities of Culture: A Global Respective*. London: Routledge.

Stevenson, D., Dunn, K., Possamai, A. and Piracha, A. (2010) Religious belief across 'post-secular' Sydney: the multiple trends in (de)secularisation. *Australian Geographer* 41(3), 323–50.

Talbot, D. (2011) The juridification of nightlife and alternative culture: two UK case studies. *International Journal of Cultural Policy* 17(1), 81–93.

Thomas, C. and Bromley, R. (2000) City-centre revitalisation: problems of fragmentation and fear in the evening and night-time city. *Urban Studies* 37(8), 1403–29.

Thrasher, F. (1927) *The Gang*. Chicago: University of Chicago Press.

Tomsen, S. (1997) A top night: social protest, masculinity and the culture of drinking violence. *British Journal of Criminology* 37(1), 90–102.

Tomsen, S. and Markwell, K. (2007) *When the Glitter Settles: Safety and Hostility at and around Gay and Lesbian Public*

*Events*. Cultural Institutions and Practices Research Centre, The University of Newcastle, Australia.

Tonkiss, F. (2005) *Space, the City and Social Theory*. Cambridge: Polity.

Tönnies, F. (1957/1887) *Community and Association* (translated by C.P. Loomies). London: Routledge and Kegan Paul.

Urry, J. (1985) Social relations, space and time. In: D. Gregory and J. Urry (eds.) *Social Relations and Spatial Structures*. Houndmills, UK: Macmillan, pp. 20–48.

Urry, J. (2005) The place of emotions within place. In: J. Davidson, L. Bondi and M. Smith (eds.) *Emotional Geographies*. Aldershot, UK: Ashgate, pp. 77–83.

Valentine, G. (1989) The geography of women's fear. *Area* 21(4), 385–90.

Valentine, G., Holloway, S. and Jayne, M. (2010) Contemporary cultures of abstinence and the nighttime economy: Muslim attitudes towards alcohol and the implications for social cohesion. *Environment and Planning A* 42(1), 8–22.

Vertinsky, P. and Bale, J. (eds.) (2004) *Sites of Sport: Space, Place, Experience*. London and New York: Routledge.

Waitt, G., Jessop, L. and Gorman-Murray, A. (2011) 'The guys in there just expect to be laid': embodied and gendered sociospatial practices of a 'night out' in Wollongong, Australia. *Gender, Place and Culture* 18(2), 255–75.

Wearing, S., Stevenson, D. and Young, T. (2010) *Tourist Cultures: Identity, Place and the Traveller*. London and New York: Sage.

Weber, M. (1950/1927) *General Economic History* (translated by F.H. Knight). Glencoe, IL: Free Press.

Weber, M. (1958/1921) *The City* (translated and edited by D. Martindale and G. Neuwirth). New York: Free Press.

Wiese, A. (2004) *Places of Their Own: African American Suburbanization in the Twentieth Century*. Chicago: University of Chicago Press.

Williams, Raymond (1961) *The Long Revolution*. London: Penguin.

Williams, Robert (2008) Darkness, deterritorialization, and social control. *Space and Culture* 11(4), 514–32.

Williamson, T., Imbroscio, D. and Alperovitz, G. (2005) The challenge of urban sprawl. In: N. Kleniewski (ed.) *Cities and Society*. Malden, MA: Blackwell, pp. 303–29.

Wilson, D. (2008) Segregation and division. In: T. Hall, P. Hubbard and J.R. Short (eds.) *The Sage Companion to the City*. London: Sage, pp. 210–30.

Wilson, E. (1992) *The Sphinx in the City: Urban Life, the Control of Disorder, and Women*. Berkeley, Los Angeles and Oxford: University of California Press.

Wilson, E. (2001) *The Contradictions of Culture: Cities, Culture, Women*. London: Sage.

Wilson, W. (1987) *The Truly Disadvantaged: The Inner City, the Underclass, and Public Policy*. Chicago: University of Chicago Press.

Wirth, L. (1927) The ghetto. *The American Journal of Sociology* 33(1), 57–71.

Wirth, L. (1928) *The Ghetto*. Chicago: University of Chicago Press.

Wirth, L. (1995) Urbanism as a way of life. In: P. Kasinitz (ed.) *Metropolis: Centre and Symbol of Our Times*. Houndmills, UK: Macmillan, pp. 58–85.

Wolff, J. (1985) The invisible *flâneuse*: women and the literature of modernity. *Theory, Culture and Society* 2(3), 37–46.

Wood, P. and Landry, C. (2008) *The Intercultural City: Planning for Diversity Advantage*. London: Earthscan.

Worpole, K. (1991) Trading places: the city workshop. In: M. Fisher and O. Owen (eds.) *Whose Cities?* London: Penguin, pp. 142–52.

Worpole, K. (1992) *Towns for People*. Buckingham: Open University Press.

Young, C., Diep, M. and Drabble, S. (2006) Living with difference? The 'cosmopolitan city' and urban reimaging in Manchester, UK. *Urban Studies* 43(10), 1687–714.

Young, M. and Willmott, P. (1962) *Family and Kinship in East London*. Harmondsworth, UK: Penguin.

Zhu, J. (2004) Local developmental state and order in China's urban development during transition. *The International Journal of Urban and Regional Research* 28(2), 424–47.

Zorbaugh, H. (1929) *The Gold Coast and the Slum*. Chicago: University of Chicago Press.

Zukin, S. (1980) A decade of the new urban sociology. *Theory and Society* 9(4), 575–601.

Zukin, S. (1989) *Loft Living: Culture and Capital in Urban Change*, 2nd edn. New Brunswick, NJ: Rutgers University Press.

Zukin, S. (1997) *The Cultures of Cities*. Cambridge, MA: Blackwell Publishers.

# Index

202 *Index*